ALTERNATIVE MODELS OF MENNONITE PASTORAL FORMATION

PAUL M. ZEHR and JIM EGLI

with responses by

Lois Barrett
Harold E. Bauman
Richard C. Detweiler
Ralph A. Lebold
Erick Sawatzky

Foreword by Ross T. Bender

OCCASIONAL PAPERS NO. 15

Institute of Mennonite Studies
3003 Benham Avenue
Elkhart, Indiana 46517-1999

1992

Occasional Papers

Occasional Papers is a publication of the Institute of Mennonite Studies and authorized by the Council of Mennonite Seminaries. The four sponsoring seminaries are Eastern Mennonite Seminary (Harrisonburg, VA), Goshen Biblical Seminary and Mennonite Biblical Seminary (Elkhart, IN), and the Mennonite Brethren Biblical Seminary (Fresno, CA). The Institute of Mennonite Studies is the research agency of the Associated Mennonite Biblical Seminaries.

Occasional Papers is released several times yearly without any pre-scribed calendar schedule. The purpose of the *Papers* is to make various types of essays available to foster dialogue in biblical, theological and practical ministry areas and to invite critical counsel from within the Mennonite theological community. While most essays will be in finished form, some may also be in a more germinal stage--released especially for purposes of testing and receiving criti-cal feedback. In accepting papers for publication, priority will be given to authors from the CMS institutions, the college Bible faculties in the Council of Mennonite Colleges, the associate mem-bership of the Institute of Mennonite Studies, and students and degree alumni of the four seminaries.

Because of limited circulation of the *Occasional Papers,* authors are free to use their material in other scholarly settings, either for oral presentation at scholarly meetings or for publication in journals with broader circulation and more official publication policies.

Orders for *Occasional Papers* should be sent to the Institute of Men-nonite Studies, 3003 Benham Avenue, Elkhart, IN 46517-1999.

ISBN 0-936273-19-4
Printed in the USA

OTHER OCCASIONAL PAPERS BY THE INSTITUTE OF MENNONITE STUDIES:

No. 1 *Biblical Essays on War, Peace and Justice*   (out of print)

No. 2 *Theological Education in Missional Perspective*   (out of print)

No. 3 *The Bible and Law*

No. 4 *Following Jesus Christ in the World Today*

No. 5 *The Pastor-People Partnership: The Call and Recall of Pastors from a Believers' Church Perspective*

No. 6 *Perspectives on the Nurturing of Faith*

No. 7 *Explorations of Systematic Theology*   (out of print)

No. 8 *Dialog Sequel to Moltmann's Following Jesus Christ in the World Today*

No. 9 *Essays on War and Peace: Bible and Early Church*

No. 10 *Perspectives on Feminist Hermeneutics*

No. 11 *Essays on Spiritual Bondage and Deliverance*

No. 12 *Essays on Peace Theology and Witness*

No. 13 *A Disciple's Christology: Appraisals of Kraus's* Jesus Christ Our Lord

No. 14 *Anabaptist-Mennonite Identities in Ferment*

No. 15 *Alternative Models of Mennonite Pastoral Formation*

To order any of these publications or to receive a complete listing of other IMS publications, please contact the Institute of Mennonite Studies, 3003 Benham Avenue, Elkhart, IN 46517-1999; 219/295-3726.

TABLE OF CONTENTS

Foreword by Ross T. Bender v

1. A Curriculum Guide for Mennonite Conference-
   Based Pastoral Education by Paul M. Zehr 1

2. Leadership Training for the Church of the Future by
   Jim Egli 41

3. Responses by   Lois Barrett 93
                          Harold E. Bauman 98
                          Richard C. Detweiler 105
                          Ralph A. Lebold 109
                          Erick Sawatzky 118

4. The Last Word by   Paul M. Zehr 125
                          Jim Egli 128

Contributors 135

FOREWORD

The decade of the 60's seems in some respects to be a long time ago. The 60's were a time of social and political ferment. They were the years when John F. Kennedy was elected, then assassinated. His brother Robert and Martin Luther King Jr. were also cut down only a few years later. The 60's were the years of the Vietnam War and the civil rights marches. They were a time when the social conscience of the nation and much of the world was raised to a high degree of awareness and sensitivity. The 60's were also a time of alienation between the generations as many youth and young adults were frustrated beyond the normal levels of tolerance and despaired of their ability to change the system.

The 60's were a time of ferment not only in society at large but in the church as well. Churches were searching for new forms of church life in response to the disaffection of youth and in response to the scathing criticism they were receiving from various sources for their institutionalization and routinization of the gospel. Churches were being criticized for their social conservatism and lack of social conscience, for their lack of leadership in the civil rights, anti-war and war against poverty movements. A number of books appeared in the 60's with such titles as *The Gathering Storm in the Churches, The Noise of Solemn Assemblies, The Suburban Captivity of the Churches, The Secular City, The Comfortable Pew.*

Mennonite churches were not immune to this ferment and to the resulting alienation between those who clung to familiar and tested ways and those who advocated change in search of relevance. All institutions, structures, conventions, patterns of leadership and theological formulations were re-examined critically, not only in the mainstream churches but also in the Mennonite churches.

The 60's were also a time of ferment in theological education. In the late 1950's, the Association of Theological Schools sponsored a study of theological education among its member schools. It was headed up by H. Richard Niebuhr, Daniel Day Williams and James Gustafson. In the several volumes which came out of that study, there was already some evidence of ferment in patterns of theological education which for many decades prior to that had consisted of courses in the disciplines of Bible, theology, church history and ethics with an additional course or two in preaching, Christian education and administration. The result of this study, however, was not only to document the existing ferment but also to let loose additional efforts at reforming the curriculum of theological studies.

There followed a whole series of studies and of curricular innovations including a study of pre-seminary education and of field education. The changes in pre-seminary education opened up admission to the theological schools (and to the Christian ministry) to persons with a wide variety of undergraduate majors (mathematics, the natural sciences, the social sciences, education, social welfare, architecture, business, and the like). In addition, a growing number of older persons who were exploring the possibility of making a mid-life career change from their various professions into the Christian ministry began to appear in the seminary student body. The social, political and intellectual ferment of which we have spoken awakened the interest of many persons in searching for answers in the Christian heritage.

These changes had significant implications for the seminary curriculum since it could no longer be presupposed that all students had a more or less common background. Nor, for that matter, could it be assumed that all students had a common professional goal, the pastoral ministry. As a result, the curriculum had to become much more diversified and flexible than it had been in the past.

Dr. Charles Fielding directed a study entitled "Education For Ministry" designed to look into patterns of supervised field education (earlier called field work) and to prepare recommendations for the future. The result was to bring supervision as an educational method into a place of central importance in the curriculum of many schools.

Even more radical changes were in store, pioneered by such schools as the University of Chicago Divinity School and the School of Theology at Clarement who launched a 4-year Doctor of Ministry program; these developments simultaneously launched a furious debate among the member schools of the Association of Theological Schools. By this time, of course, the D.Min. degree has proven itself and won its way. Standards for accrediting these programs have been agreed upon and many schools are now offering this degree.

In 1966, the ATS set up a committee on resources in theological education. The word went out that in the future there would be fewer centers of theological education in North America (perhaps as few as twenty-five); that these centers would be ecumenical in character; and that they would be affiliated in clusters, attached to the graduate schools of the major universities in Canada and the United States.

Needless to say, this caused both excitement and consternation among the smaller denominational schools, including the Associated Mennonite Biblical Seminaries. These are among the factors which led to setting up the study project to develop a model for theological education in the Free Church tradition. The project was based on the conviction that there is in our heritage a distinctive understanding of the nature of the church and the church's ministry which should shape the patterns of church life, of ministry and of theological education for our time. It was in the midst of the ferment which I have briefly described that we set out on our quest.[1]

At the same time there were developments outside the AMBS community which would have a significant impact on the way Mennonite pastors were being equipped for ministry. Several congregations in Ontario, Manitoba and Kansas offered yearlong internships to seminarians for which AMBS gave academic credit. There was usually a unit of Clinical Pastoral Education (called Supervised Pastoral Education in Canada) available in a nearby hospital setting.

These early efforts eventually grew into what is today called Conference-Based Theological Education. There are now seven approved CBTE centers in the Mennonite church. Academic credit is given by AMBS and Eastern Mennonite Seminary. They are as follows (with the name of the director in parentheses):

The Pastoral Leadership Training Commission is sponsored by the Mennonite Conference of Eastern Canada (Ralph A. Lebold).

The Great Plains Seminary Education Program is sponsored by the South Central Conference of the Mennonite Church and the Western District of the General Conference Mennonite Church (Jacob T. Friesen).

The Mennonites in Illinois Leadership Education (MILE) Program is sponsored by the western portion of the Central District of the General Conference Mennonite Church and the Illinois Mennonite Conference of the Mennonite Church (Conrad Wetzel).

The Inter-Conference Pastoral Training Board is sponsored by the Atlantic Coast, the Franconia and the Lancaster Mennonite Conferences of the Mennonite Church (Ross Goldfus, Richard C. Detweiler, now deceased, and Paul M. Zehr respectively).

The Congregational Leadership Training Program is sponsored by the Virginia Mennonite Conference of the Mennonite Church (Sam Weaver).

Several additional programs are in various stages of development including one in the Southeast Mennonite Conference under the leadership of Leroy Bechler.

The first major essay in this issue, "A Curriculum Guide for Mennonite Conference-Based Pastoral Education", written by Paul M. Zehr describes the philosophy, objectives and curriculum of the Lancaster Mennonite Conference program of which Paul Zehr is the director. It is an abbreviated version of Zehr's thesis- project for the Doctor of Ministry degree presented to the faculty of Eastern Baptist Theological Seminary (April 1987). In the original version, Zehr reports on extension programs in theological education including TEE (Theological Education by Extension), a program in wide and effective use in many third world settings, as well as experience-based learning approaches of which Clinical Pastoral Education is a leading example. He also outlines in some detail the curriculum of the Lancaster Conference program.

The second paper, "Leadership Training for the Church of the Future", written by Jim Egli, goes further in its critique of Mennonite seminary education than Zehr's paper does. Conference-Based Theological Education does not attempt to compete with Seminary-Based Theological Education. It assumes a complementary role, providing similar kinds of educational opportunities to those found on the seminary campus for persons already in the pastoral ministry without requiring them to leave their homes and their congregations to study at a seminary. The seminaries accredit these programs and offer transcript credit for their work. These credits qualify the student to graduate with a seminary degree, usually on the basis of some additional work done "in residence".

Jim Egli's model will have none of this. He makes the point that Jesus and Paul both rejected the residential, academic model of equipping disciples for Christian ministry in favor of an approach which emphasized learning in the midst of actual engagement in ministry under supervision. While Jesus' curriculum contained cognitive material, he emphasized the relational dimension- with God, with each other, with the people to whom they were ministering.

In a letter responding to my proposal to call this publication "Alternative Models of Mennonite Theological Education", Egli stated, "One problem I see with 'Alternative Models of Mennonite Theological Education' is that 'Theological Education' implies that the academic/cognitive dimension is at the core of the process. The point of the TEE movement and much of the other rethinking that is taking place now is that the cognitive dimension is only part of the picture and that it must be thoroughly integrated with the relational elements of prayer, mentoring and ministry involvement to be effective. I would prefer a title that more clearly implies that."

Egli's paper, also an abbreviated version of his master's thesis at Lincoln Theological Seminary in Illinois, is a hard-hitting critique of the academic, residential approach to theological education found in most if not all seminaries by the very nature of their enterprise. He offers not a supplement or a satellite approach but a completely new approach which bypasses the seminary model altogether. Whatever the reader may conclude about the answers Egli provides, s/he will be stimulated to think again about the nature of the task of equipping Christian ministers to be effective in their calling.

We offer these two presentations, one innovative and the other iconoclastic, to our readers together with the responses of several thoughtful observers who have taken time to read the manuscripts and to offer their reflections on a timely subject. Although Paul Zehr and Jim Egli have been invited to have the last word by replying to the respondents, the last word has yet to be spoken on a subject of lively interest to many people.

Ross T. Bender, Director
Institute of Mennonite Studies
Elkhart, Indiana

ENDNOTE

1. For a full report on the study project to develop a model for theological education in the Free Church tradition, see Ross T. Bender, The People of God: A Mennonite Interpretation of the Free Church Tradition (Scottdale, PA: Herald Press, 1971).

CONTRIBUTORS

Ross T. Bender, who edited this volume, is the Director of the Institute of Mennonite Studies. Earlier he served as Dean of the Associated Mennonite Biblical Seminaries.

Jim Egli is pastor of the Flanagan Mennonite Church, Illinois, a member of the Central District of the General Conference Mennonite Church. He also serves part-time as Project Coordinator for LIFE (Living in Faithful Evangelism), a three-year growth process for congregations. LIFE is a joint project of the Mennonite Church and the General Conference Mennonite Church.

Paul M. Zehr is the Director of the Lancaster Campus of Eastern Mennonite College and Seminary. He directs the Lancaster Mennonite Conference Pastoral Education Program which includes a Foundation Studies Program, Supervised Pastoral Education and Continuing Education.

Lois Barrett is co-pastor of the Mennonite Church of the Servant in Wichita, Kansas and teaches part-time in the Great Plains Seminary Education Program. She is a PhD candidate in Historical Theology at the Union Institute, Cincinnati, Ohio.

Harold E. Bauman recently retired as the Director of the Ministerial Information Service and as a staff member of the Mennonite Board of Congregational Ministries.

Richard C. Detweiler was the Director of Pastoral Training for the Franconia Mennonite Conference until his death in the late summer of 1991. Formerly he served as President of Eastern Mennonite College and Seminary

Ralph A. Lebold is Director of Pastoral Leadership Training for the Mennonite Conference of Eastern Canada and Director of External Programs for the Associated Mennonite Biblical Seminaries. Formerly he served as President of Conrad Grebel College.

Erick Sawatzky is Assistant Professor of Pastoral Ministry and Director of Field Education at the Associated Mennonite Biblical Seminaries. He has served as a pastor in both the USA and Canada; from 1981-85, he was the executive director of the Saskatoon Pastoral Institute.

Chapter 1

A Curriculum Guide for Mennonite Conference-Based Pastoral Education

Paul M. Zehr

Introduction

Presently over 70% of the ordained and licensed leaders in the Mennonite Church congregations are pastoring without the benefit of seminary education.[1] Mennonite seminaries are doing a commendable job in educating the remaining 25% of Mennonite Church pastors, but who will train the many bivocational pastors who have not attended seminary and what kind of training program is needed?

Conference-Based Pastoral Education began in 1980 in Lancaster Mennonite Conference as one way to train its pastors. It is designed to equip the following for ministry more fully:

- persons already serving in a leadership role without training
- new person who will be ordained or licensed as bishops, ministers, and deacons
- persons with college and/or seminary training who desire continuing education for growth in their ministry
- persons who sense a call to ministry and who are identified as potential leaders who wish to test their interest or gifts.

Four major questions arise in regard to training for the pastoral ministry.

1) What must a pastor *be* in order to be an effective minister? This question points to the importance of the pastor's own spiritual life and personality as a major ingredient of congregational leadership.

2) What must the pastor *know* in order to be an effective minister? What kind of knowledge and how much is needed to pastor effectively in today's world?

3) What must the pastor *do* to be an effective minister? What skills are needed for the pastoral ministry and how shall they be developed?

4) Finally, what attitude must the pastor exercise in the ministry to be effective?

Four major studies comprise the background out of which the curriculum guide emerged: biblical/theological study of the pastoral gift in the congregation, Mennonite philosophy of education, extension programs in theological education, and experience-based learning.

1. Biblical/Theological Study of the Pastoral Gift in the Congregation

In the epistles gifts and grace become a dominant theme in regard to leadership in the early church, particularly Ephesians. Ephesians 4:7-16 finds its place alongside the list of gifts in I Corinthians 12:8-10; I Corinthians 12:28-30; Romans 12:6-8; and I Peter 4:10. These *charismata* are given for the good of the total Christian community. The ascended Lord gifts the church to carry out its task in the world. The non-office and office gifts function together in a unified way both to bring unity within the body of Christ and to enhance the church's ministry toward the world. The Ephesians 4:7-16 text indicates the ordering of the church is not by democracy whereby the leaders carry out the will of the people. Rather it is a Christocracy in which the rule of Christ in the gathered Christian community finds expression. Implicit in this view is both the placement of leaders, including the pastor, and the function of leaders, namely, to call the people to the will of Christ who is the head of the church.

Paul identifies apostles, prophets, evangelists, pastors and teachers. Of particular interest is the Greek text in Ephesians 4:12. Many English translations place a comma after the word saints in verse 12. But as Markus Barth points out:

> The meaning of 4:12 is entirely different when the nouns preceded by different prepositions describe one and the same purpose of the ministries mentioned in verse 11, and when no comma is placed between the first two parts of verse 12. Then the ministries of verse 11 are given to the church in order that 'the saints' become 'equipped' to carry out 'the work of service', even 'the building' ... Ephesians 4:12 may indeed underline the fact that the 'saints' are not a part of the church but all her members, without excluding any one of them. All the saints (and among them, each saint) are enabled by the four or five types of servants enumerated in 4:11 to fulfill the ministry given to them so that the whole church is taken into Christ's service and given missionary substance, purpose and structure.[2]

In short, the function of the pastoral gift is to equip members for mission and service. To move in the direction of a theologically educated congregation equipped for service in the world requires a major change in the way pastors are educated. Pastoral education has traditionally reflected a clerical paradigm rather than a congregational paradigm.[3] This orientation has resulted in the neglect of theological education in the congregation and leads to a theologically literate clergy and a theologically illiterate laity. Edward Farley asks:

> How is it possible one can attend or even teach in a Sunday school for decades, and at the end of that time lack the interpretive skills of someone who has taken three or four weeks in an introductory course in Bible at a university or seminary?[4]

One wonders what direction pastoral education might take if the paradigm is shifted, as Eph. 4:7-16 suggests, from the clergy to the congregation and the pastor's task is to bring about a redemptive community that is theologically literate and equipped to minister inside and outside the congregation.

This pastor-teacher-equipper role goes beyond the prophetic view of ministry, reflected in Protestantism, which interprets preaching as the moment when the grace of God is received through God's spoken word.[5] It also goes beyond the sacramental view of ministry, seen in Catholicism, by which the power and grace of God are released through the sacraments.[6] The pastor-teacher-equipper view of ministry can also be distinguished from the kingly view of ministry seen in Charismatic and Fundamentalistic circles. It is not the same as the priestly view of ministry seen in some contemporary interpretations of the minister as therapist. Following the medical model the pastor is seen as pathologist who listens to people's pain and prescribes a healing word of counsel. Too much attention is given to pathology rather than the development of a healthy spiritual membership which is equipped for service in the world.

The pastor-teacher-equipper leads the congregation in its spiritual development by his/her own spiritual life, by opening the meaning of scripture through good biblical preaching, through a teaching program that leads the congregation into the depths of God's Word and the meaning of Christian theology today, and by developing skills for ministry and service in the world through special training efforts and an effective administration of the congregation in its mission.

2. Mennonite Philosophy of Education

Not until the 1960s did the Mennonite Board of Education

develop a major statement on a philosophy of education.[7] During those same years the Associated Mennonite Biblical Seminaries developed a philosophy of Theological Education in the Free Church Tradition.[8] However, some evidence of an underlying philosophy is found previously in Mennonite history.

The Anabaptists emphasized the quality of the pastor's spiritual life. Partially in reaction to the Christian movements of the 16th century and partially due to the influence of humanism, the Anabaptists sought for moral reform.[9] Coupled with an emphasis on discipleship, the Anabaptists called for new life in Jesus Christ which obeyed Christ in the midst of life. Both in the statement of faith at Schleitheim in 1527 and at Dordrecht in 1632 attention is called to the spiritual qualities of the congregational leader rather than intellectual abilities or even skills for ministry. Anabaptism reflects more of a Hebraic than a Greek philosophy of education. The whole life was to be brought literally under the lordship of Jesus Christ and one was to live out his/her faith in the context of Christian community.

The Mennonite Church in North America did not begin seminary training until after World War II. However, as early as 1923, Harold S. Bender encouraged leadership training to help keep its youth within the church, meet the challenges of the day, move out into mission, and maintain its peace doctrine.[10]

The Mennonite Board of Education philosophy of education calls for identity, peoplehood as part of God's movement in history, and learning within Christian community as important ingredients of Mennonite education. As part of the AMBS study J. Lawrence Burkholder raised major concerns about theological education by noting that most Protestant seminaries have a relatively uniform pattern of theological education and have not taken into consideration the denomination's theology and context of ministry. Burkholder wrote,

> Although many of our denominational seminaries were established in the 19th century for the purpose of defending and promoting particular theologies, it is noteworthy that all seem to agree on what it takes to educate for the ministry. It has been agreed by Episcopalians, Presbyterians, Baptists, and now by Mennonites, that it takes precisely three years beyond college, no more, no less, for everyone, regardless of who he is, and whether he plans to minister to the hill folk of Kentucky or the matrons of Madison Avenue, and regardless of whether the church is conceived as a sacramental institution or a pilgrim fellowship.[11]

In 1985 Edward Farley raised serious questions about the nature of theological education and the resultant distance between a professional clergy and lay person in the congregation. He concludes one cause of the dichotomy is the European university model undergirding western theological education.[12] The AMBS study, led by Ross T. Bender, pointed to a Hebraic philosophy and the Christian community undergirding a Mennonite understanding of education which, in turn, considers both the content and the context of education. Bender wrote,

> Out of the study project to develop a model for theological education in the Free Church tradition has emerged the conviction that not only the *content* but also the *context* of the curriculum must be shaped by our theological convictions. At the very heart of the Free Church commitment is the understanding of the church as a covenant community. The central shaping reality for the program of theological education is the purpose of God in history to create a people for himself. The organizing principle of the curriculum is the attempt to discover and to realize what it is to be faithful people of God now--what forms that peoplehood should take in the congregations and in the seminary--with a view to setting up program and structures that are an appropriate expression of the guiding vision.

> The context for theological education is, therefore, not first of all the university but the community of faith. The theological school stands, to be sure, in the academic tradition as well as in the ecclesiastical tradition; however it is the Judaeo-Christian tradition (as expressed through the Free Churches in this instance) rather than western culture (which forms the intellectual environment of the university) which is the true home of theological education. In short we look to Jerusalem rather than to Athens in shaping the form, substance, and style of our enterprise.[13]

In short a Mennonite philosophy of pastoral education includes the following:

1) It is first of all Christian education. Pastors are educated to understand God, the person and work of Jesus Christ, salvation for humankind, the Holy Spirit, the church, and eschatology. It includes biblical studies, theological studies, historical studies, and Christian ethics.

2) It has as its object training pastors to lead congregations of contemporary people of God in the believers' church context. Here pastors discover who they are and their purpose within the context of human history.

3) It reflects a Hebraic philosophy of life in which the will and total person is called to obey Christ. Students and pastors are called first to obedience and secondly to academic achievement.

4) It includes spiritual formation. Mennonite pastors lead by modeling Christian discipleship. It develops the pastor's spiritual life along with cognitive understandings of theology and ministry skills.

5) It is oriented to the faith community. Students learn in the context of Christian community and prepare to minister alongside other gifted persons in the congregation.

6) It is contextual. Pastors learn how to understand their context of ministry in order to apply the gospel to their given cultural setting.

7) It involves training both pastors and lay leaders so that both the professional and nonprofessional can work together in ministry and both can freely exercise their spiritual gifts in the total ministry of the congregation.

8) It is academic in that it gives the student an intellectual understanding of the Bible, theology, and the history of the Christian movement including Anabaptist theology and history.

9) It is professional in that personal skills are developed for preaching, teaching, pastoral care and counseling, administration, and evangelism.

10) It includes supervised experience in ministry by which ministry skills are developed.

11) It is training through the various stages of the pastoral ministry including preordination, early ministry, middle years of ministry, and finally the late years of ministry.

12) Mennonite pastoral education after ordination and beyond the seminary level is tailored to meet the individual pastor's needs.

13) It includes self learning by observing others in ministry, exercising good reading habits, attending seminars, etc.

14) It includes both training to lead the congregation of God's people and training to relate to people.

15) It is functional in character in that pastoral training has as its primary purpose leading the congregation into a life of Christian commitment and obedience. This means the pastor's intellectual pursuits are directed toward ministry rather than academia alone.

16) It is mission oriented in that its goal is to produce pastors who in turn enable the congregation's members to carry out mission and service in the world.

3. Extension Programs in Theological Education

Due to the growth of the church, leadership training is at the forefront of mission activity. However, missionaries discovered difficulty in transferring western seminary models of education to the third world. Traditional western seminary education, it was found, has the following problems:

1) It tends to be pre-clinical. Whereas, education in law, business, and medicine focuses in part on theory, major attention is given to practice. In contrast seminary education rests largely on the pre-clinical years.

2) Western seminary education is too expensive for third world churches. Due to a low student/faculty ratio and the small size of the average seminary, it is very expensive.

3) Western seminary education tends to create a dichotomy between the educated pastor and uneducated laity in the third world churches.

4) The western seminary graduate finds it difficult to adjust to the cultural milieu of the third world.

5) Western seminary graduates often come to the congregation without tested leadership ability and experience.

6) Third world churches face a shortage of trained pastors because western seminaries produce too few graduates to meet the rapid growth of younger churches.

7) Third world churches want pastors to mobilize the congregation for mission.

Because of these deficiencies, missionaries longed for a new method of training national pastors. Theological Education by Extension (TEE) was born in Guatemala in 1962. After 25 years of educating pastors in a seminary in Guatemala City by the Presbyterian Church, only 10 of the 200 seminary graduates still functioned as pastors.[14] Recognizing the problem, a decision was made to decentralize theological education by arranging for regional centers and having the seminary teachers meet weekly with students in those regional centers. The method worked so well that in 1963 the residential seminary was suspended and with no increase in personnel or funds this decentralized effort expanded the enrollment from 7 to more than 200 by 1966. Reflecting on the experiment Kinsler wrote,

> In four years the enrollment grew from six to two hundred; the students now remain in their varied contexts and study part-time; they do not become economically dependent on

the churches either for their studies or for future services; they are generally mature, experienced leaders; and they are able to relate theological studies to ministerial practice as never before.[15]

TEE grew rapidly in Central America, South America, Africa, and Asia. Writing in 1983, F. Ross Kinsler reported,

> The numerical and geographical expansion of the extension movement from a handful of experiments in Latin America at the end of the 1960s to 300 to 400 programs with perhaps 10,000 students around the world at the end of the 1970s has been extraordinary. During this decade the initiative of the extension movement has passed from small, marginal, ill-equipped schemes led by expatriate missionaries to large, well-endowed efforts run by major theological institutions and prompted by associations of theological schools...The cumulative effect of all these developments is difficult to evaluate at this stage, but present indications are that escalation will continue at least through the 1980s.[16]

Writing in 1984, David Kornfield identified the continuing advantages of TEE as follows:

1) It allows for the training of many more students with the same faculty.
2) It trains the real leaders of the local church who are already manifesting their spiritual gifts and have proven God's call on their life.
3) It leaves the leader where one is needed during one's training.
4) It allows people tied down by work and family to receive training.
5) It occurs in the context of the student's future place of ministry.
6) It encourages the practice of self-study.
7) Problems and needs in the learner's ministry will stimulate learning to discover answers.
8) It encourages tent-making ministries in small churches.
9) It can be used to train people of varied cultural backgrounds.
10) It provides education of a quality at least equal with residential seminary programs, perhaps superior in terms of preparing a person to minister in a particular place.

11) It can produce almost immediate observable results in the local church.

12) And it is cheaper.[17]

TEE educational philosophy, like Anabaptist/Mennonite education, reflects a Hebraic view. Through the influence of Paulo Freire, attention is focused upon person-centered learning by which the person relates content to one's actual situation in life. Traditional western seminary education is limited in that it does not know how the student carries out ministry in his/her environment. Corvell and Wagner note,

> The traditional school does not afford us a good context to evaluate the total life of the student. We are able to tell how he does in his courses, how he is able to articulate, whether he does better on an objective text or on an essay test, and whether or not he turns assignments in on time...However, we often know little about many things that will cause him to succeed or fail in his ministry.

> Theological Education by Extension affords a better context in which to evaluate the student. Those being trained are mature leaders already working in the church. They are educated in an environment closely related to the church. Therefore, the evaluation can easily be done by members of the church in which they are serving. This evaluation is much more complete, because the church is able to see the student in the total environment in which he is living.[18]

TEE seeks to integrate experience and academic studies. Ted Ward uses the analogy of the split-rail fence to describe the educational philosophy of TEE. The upper rail represents cognitive input; the lower rail represents field experience, and the fence post represents seminars designed to relate cognitive input to field experience.[19]

TEE seeks to contextualize theological education so that it is relevant to the pastor where she/he is located. Students learn within their own context of ministry.

It includes programmed textbooks which are prepared for given cultural settings. A lesson often comprises three essential elements: the course content is ordered in a logical and progressive manner so as to facilitate the learning process by moving from the simple to the complex, what is learned is applied immediately through a step by step process involving exercises and solving problems, and the student checks his use of the new knowledge point by point to reinforce what he has learned. In addition, a weekly seminar is held with a teacher in which the material is reviewed to explore the meanings, implications, and applications of the material.

TEE enables students to learn more effectively in their own language, attracts persons across the life span, concentrates on those who are already leaders, reaches persons at different academic levels, offers training for any person in the congregation who desires it, thus unifying clergy and lay persons.

Geographically speaking, TEE takes education to the pastors rather than taking pastors to the seminary. Economically, TEE trains persons where the family is already making its living instead of uprooting the family and paying a huge sum of money to study at a seminary. Sociologically, TEE appeals to persons at many cultural and educational levels.[20] TEE in short is a field-based approach which does not interrupt the learner's productive relationship to society. Its purpose is to extend theological education to the real leaders of the local congregations, thus enabling them to develop their gifts and ministries in order to participate more fully and effectively in the life and growth of the church.[21]

Building on TEE insights, the Mennonite churches in Central America have developed a training program known as SEMILLA (Seminario Ministerial de Liderazgo Anabautista-Menonita) which seeks to train congregational leaders in the midst of their cultural context from an Anabaptist theological perspective.

Here in North America debate continues between leaders of traditional western seminary education and others involved in extension education. Barbara Wheeler, President of Auburn Theological Seminary in New York City, is not optimistic about extension education and feels the professionalism of American culture will not accept extension education as its norm. Others feel differently. For example, New York Theological Seminary changed its entire approach when it declined in the 1960s. The seminary decided to create a special education program for clergy and lay leaders serving churches in the greater New York City metropolitan area. Programs were designed to aid pastors in competency for ministry rather than merely teaching the theological disciplines. As a result of this new direction, enrollment has increased dramatically to well over 700 students with multiple training programs designed to meet the needs of persons involved in ministry in the churches.

Other extension programs include the Episcopal school of the University of the South with 4,000 students, the Southern Baptist Seminary with 11,000 students, and San Francisco Seminary with several locations on the west coast.

From this study of extension programs in theological education, the following implications are drawn for conference-based pastoral education:

1) A decentralized model of pastoral education can be viable and academically sound.

2) Curriculum for pastoral training requires a contextual element by which students relate their learning to the actual experience of ministry in the congregation.

3) From TEE and NYTS it is possible to develop a model of education that is practical, fits the pastor in his/her present work arrangement, and is affordable.

4) Curriculum can be developed that includes a combination of home study and classes or seminars.

5) Flexibility in education is possible so that classes or seminars can be scheduled outside the regular 8:00 a.m. to 5:00 p.m. Monday through Friday work week.

6) Curriculum can be designed to meet a diversity of age levels, academic levels, and levels of involvement in congregational life.

7) A decentralized curriculum needs balance between the felt needs of the student, actual needs of the congregation, and the larger biblical, historical, theological, and practical studies of ministry.

8) TEE and other extension programs indicate it is possible to integrate the academic and the professional in pastoral education.

4. Experience-Based Learning

In 1925 Clinical Pastoral Education (CPE) emerged as experience-based learning. It was begun at Worcester State Hospital in New England in the summer of 1925 by Anton T. Boisen. Boisen approached theology by the route of anthropology, particularly humankind in mental and physical illness. He believed that one can observe persons in the midst of crisis and discover new insights into the meaning of theology and faith.

Though the movement was inundated with conflict between the years of 1930 and 1946,[22] it survived largely through the influence of Seward Hiltner who emphasized the dialogue between the behavioral sciences and theology.

After World War II the movement spread with new centers starting all over the U.S.A. In 1949 the Lutherans began a CPE program and in 1957 the Southern Baptists likewise began a CPE program. In 1967 four national groups moved closer together and formed the Association of Clinical Pastoral Education, Inc. (ACPE) including a constitution and bylaws.[23]

Four stages of development are distinguishable in the CPE movement.[24] From 1925 to 1935 the basic question was, What must I do to be of help to the patient? From 1935 to 1945 the basic question changed to, What must I know to be of help to the patient? From 1945 to 1955 the basic question became, What must I say to be of help to the patient? Then from 1955 to 1965 the CPE supervisors and students began to ask, What must I be to be of help to the patient? Today CPE concerns itself with an interplay between these four questions.

Anton T. Boisen believed that if one observes "the living human document" and studies the way human beings think, feel, and act during crisis one can begin to determine how theology interacts with human life. CPE enables the church to learn from human experience alongside learning from the documents of the church and its theologians. Thus a major ingredient of CPE education is the living human document. Another ingredient is the case method in which one listens to the person's case history, including religious life, to gain insight into factors affecting human behavior.

A third ingredient is the verbatim, borrowed by Russel Dicks from social scientists, in which one records the conversation between the pastor and the patient in an attempt to learn what the minister and the patient mean in the conversation and how well that meaning is or is not received by the other person.

Finally, CPE is supervised encounter. Persons are trained often in hospital settings under supervision. The pastor reports regularly on his/her work and receives feedback from a supervisor. Experience-based learning under supervision enables pastors or seminary students to become aware of who they are and how they relate to other persons. Whereas academic studies focus upon the cognitive, CPE gives attention to the relational. Basic to an understanding of the goals of CPE then, according to Thompson,

> is the realization that pastoral ministry is firstly "being" and the gift one brings is one's own person. Clearly the emphasis then in pastoral ministry is on interpersonal relationships.[25]

CPE utilizes an action/reflection method of learning. The pastor does an act of ministry and then reflects upon it. In reflection the pastor analyzes what is going on theologically, ethically, socially, and spiritually during the encounter between the patient and the pastor. Students also formulate their own learning goals which in turn become a device to evaluate the student's progress. CPE learning, then, is behavioral in nature by its use of a selfdirected learning model.

Despite major progress and wide acceptance of CPE since 1967, problems continue to plague the movement. One problem is the philosophical background affecting the development of the CPE movement. In the late 1930s and the 1940s the CPE movement divided between the Robert E. Brinkman influence which emphasized science subsuming theology and the Seward Hiltner influence which stressed theological thinking about human experience.[26] As Hammett points out, the underlying issue throughout the twentieth century with CPE is the interfacing of scientific inquiry and theology.[27]

A second area of concern is the ethical assumptions underlying CPE programs and the pastoral care movement. Don S. Browning has called for a greater emphasis on moral behavior in contemporary Christianity. He criticizes modern psychotherapy for instructing pastors not to moralize in counseling.[28]

A third area of concern is whether CPE is theological education or therapy.[29] Seward Hiltner is to be credited with keeping CPE in the theological education camp. Hiltner felt psychotherapy should be done by mental health specialists and that the minister should provide pastoral support and deal with religious issues but not become a psychotherapist. Voices such as William H. Willimon continue to call CPE to theological education.[30]

CPE (SPE in Canada) is primarily hospital-based as noted above. There have been attempts, however, to develop a CPE program in a parish setting. Encouraged by Ernest E. Bruder, Rev. Robert K. Nace began a parish CPE program at Zion Reformed-United Church of Christ in Greenville, Pennsylvania in September of 1965. After supervising pastors for several years in this parish-based setting, Nace's major discovery

> is that the distinction between the "parish model" and the "institutional model" of CPE is in fact a distinction in the definition of the living human document around which CPE occurs.[31]

Building on Nace's adventure, Rev. Robert E. Thompson began a parish-based SPE program in 1984 at 725 member Northlea United Church in Toronto, Canada. Thompson served as pastor of the congregation and supervisor of the SPE program. From May through July, 1984 he supervised six students for twelve full weeks, giving them one full unit of SPE, in a context where all the pastor's acts of ministry take place. From the experience of these two parish-based programs, the following differences between a parish-based and an institutional-based program are discernible:

1) There is a new context for learning. Should pastoral training take place in a restricted context of people's lives or in a more generalized context? Should the pastor be trained where only a small portion of his/her ministry takes place, important as it is, or should training take place in the parish setting where all of his/her ministry takes place? CPE programs that are based in the parish actually provide a wider context for learning since all of the pastor's acts of ministry can be observed.

2) There is a change in the living human document and a change of persons in the dialogue. Nace notes two major changes:

> The first is that the "living human document" of parish CPE is no longer the person in "crisis and/or pathology" but rather the person in the normal, routine pilgrimage of life (granted there is crisis in pathology in the parish as well as in the institution, but this is no longer the focus of attention and identification).

> Secondly, the "persons" in the CPE dialogue change. Whereas in institutional CPE the dialogue is primarily one-to-one between the student and the "patient," in parish CPE this dialogue is more complex and includes three different "persons." There is (1) one-to-one dialogue between the pastor and the parishioner; (2) there is dialogue between the pastor and the total congregation as a living human unit with its unique character, history, defenses, etc.; and (3) there is a dialogue between the total congregation (including the pastors) and the community in which the congregation lives, moves, and ministers.[32]

In short, the parish itself becomes the living human document and the pastor works with this larger living organism including the pastor's relationship to the people, the people's relationship to God, the people's relationship to each other, and the people's relationship to persons outside the church.

3) There is a change of emphasis from pathology to development. Perhaps the greatest difference between hospital and parish-based CPE is the fact that ministry changes from pathology (helping the patient get well) to development and growth for persons in the congregation. Hospital-based CPE may cause pastors to view members in the congregation as "sick" and transfer a pathological emphasis to the congregation. Archie MacLachlan says,

It seems to me that the training that is going on in institutions is limited in its ability to train people for ministry. It is institutionally bound. Institutions are pathology oriented, they are concerned with healing-restoring ability to cope with life--they are not oriented to the prevention of pathology, personal or social--they are not geared to facilitating normal growth and development. They serve to get people back into circulation, but they are not oriented to giving people the basic motivation necessary for inspired and inspiring creative life.[33]

This survey of the CPE movement and recent attempts to develop parish-based CPE programs leads to the following observations:

1) CPE brings new insights into the way people experience God's work in their lives as the pastor observes the living human document in the midst of crisis. These insights otherwise are largely unknown.

2) CPE has contributed much to theological education through its emphasis on the integration of theology and the behavioral sciences.

3) The CPE action/reflection educational method in the context of peers under supervision helps pastors learn as they receive feedback on their relational skills, listening skills, and counseling skills.

4) Possibilities exist for moving the context of CPE training from institutions to the parish setting. If new ways can be found for students to participate in parish life, from which a normal living human document is available for observation rather than one in crisis with its resultant emphasis on pathology, education can take place that greatly enriches student insights into the pastoral ministry. CPE has possibilities for Conference-Based Pastoral Training if its basic attention is on the development of the congregation as the living human document in the pastoral ministry rather than on therapy and psychiatry.

5) Parish-based CPE offers possibilities for training for the wider pastoral ministry including preaching, teaching, administration, evangelism, and pastoral care.

6) CPE has possibilities for Conference-Based Pastoral Education if its philosophical base is biblically grounded and if it includes an emphasis on the moral and ethical dimensions of Christian discipleship.

7) CPE as experience-based learning enables the growing pastor to receive feedback on his/her work and become aware of

who he/she is as a pastor, to discover the nature of his/her relational skills, and to gain new insights into ways congregations integrate theology in the midst of human life.

5. Curriculum Guide

The preceding sections have provided a foundation for a curriculum guide for Mennonite Conference-Based Pastoral Education. Given the Lancaster Mennonite Conference setting and new ways to work at pastoral education found in the preceding sections, the following curriculum guide is recommended for training bivocational pastors in Lancaster Mennonite Conference.

This pastoral education endeavor begins with a needs assessment of each student through career and academic counseling. An assessment of the individual student's specific needs will be done through personal counseling and by making contact with key leaders in the congregation for the purpose of determining the congregation's assessment of the student's needs. Students will be encouraged to select courses on the basis of what results in good pastoral leadership in the congregation and on the basis of individual needs.

Scope
A multidimensional form of pastoral education is set forth. This curriculum guide combines a traditional classroom educational model with a semidecentralized model adapted from Theological Education by Extension. The model also incorporates elements of Supervised Pastoral Education which are adjusted to a congregational base. The curriculum is designed to reach pastors and key lay leaders of varying ages with the underlying assumption that years of pastoral experience enhance the discussion of practical aspects of the pastoral ministry. The curriculum also assumes persons will come to the studies with varying levels of academic achievement. Finally, the curriculum is designed so that a variety of geographical settings may be utilized, if necessary, in the conference's pastoral education program. Given the Lancaster setting, this curriculum assumes an adult education program will accompany it. The adult education program develops the ministry of lay persons in the congregation.

Content
Regarding content, the curriculum is designed for the Christian ministry. It emphasizes the centrality of Christ and the Holy Scriptures as the spiritual content of the Christian ministry. It views the pastor as the key person in the Christian ministry who needs certain

skills to carry out this work and to equip the congregation's members for mission in the world. It includes the spiritual formation of the Christian minister and the demands of Christian discipleship so that the minister *models* the Christian way for the congregation's members.

The curriculum gives attention to *knowledge* of Christ and the Scriptures, the history of the people of God, and where Mennonite pastors and congregations fit into that history. It enhances knowledge of the unfolding of theology in the Scriptures and its various interpretations throughout the history of the church including an Anabaptist interpretation and its place in contemporary theological discussion.

The curriculum seeks to develop the student's *skills* for the pastoral ministry. It not only gives the student insights into his/her work, but helps the student become aware of who he/she is among the people of God and of his/her task in enabling the congregation for mission in the world.

The curriculum also creates positive *attitudes* toward the Christian ministry as individual pastors develop confidence in themselves and God for the task of ministry, appreciate the Christian message more, and find new joy in working with people and observing the development of the congregation.

Context

The context of this semidecentralized educational curriculum enables the pastor to learn within the Christian community in which he/she belongs. The curriculum assumes the student will be actively involved in his/her congregation during the period of study and will relate learnings to experience of ministry in the congregation. While some of the program includes a classroom academic type of education, the student maintains weekly contact with his/her congregation to encourage the integration of academic study and experience. The curriculum assumes learning takes place in the context of one's social and cultural setting. In the Christian community one learns both through academic studies and through relationships with peers and fellow believers in the congregation. One also learns how to apply the Christian message by analyzing one's own social and cultural setting as the social context of ministry. Thus the curriculum enables the student to continue to live in his/her cultural setting, to continue to be actively involved in his/her congregation, and to continue employment, if necessary, to meet the financial needs of the family.

Faculty

This curriculum assumes teachers will be selected who are experienced in the pastoral ministry and can relate course content to congregational life. It also assumes faculty members will move beyond traditional methods of teaching to innovative and creative ways of conducting the class session that result in high student motivation for learning.

Methodology

This curriculum integrates cognitive learnings through a Foundation Series Program with learnings gained by experience in the practice of ministry. Knowledge gained in course work is reflected upon through the eyes of one's experience in ministry so that the class hour is stimulated by a combination of cognitive and experiential insights. In the Supervised Pastoral Education Program, designed for those who have completed the Foundation Studies Program and/or seminary, one's action in ministry is followed by reflection in the context of peers under supervision. Finally, the curriculum includes Continuing Education to meet the felt needs of the pastor as they arise throughout his/her ministry in the church.

With its Christian community emphasis, this curriculum reflects a Hebraic orientation in keeping with Anabaptist/Mennonite theology. A Hebraic philosophy emphasizes covenant community (Ex. 19-24). Educationally speaking this has an effect both on the content and the context of education. Learning takes into consideration the purpose of God in history, namely, to create a people for himself, and what it means to be God's people now.[34] A Hebraic philosophy also affects the context of learning. The Judeo-Christian tradition, rather than western culture reflected in the university environment, becomes the context of learning because one learns by association with students and faculty peers in Christian community as well as by reading books.[35] A Hebraic philosophy also emphasizes obedience to God as an important ingredient of learning. As Israel was called to obey Yahweh (Ex. 19-20), so Jesus invited his followers to obey to know the truth (Jn. 8:31-32). This Hebraic philosophy, as seen in Anabaptism, indicates an epistemology of obedience.[36] In short a Hebraic philosophy invites both teacher and student to Jerusalem rather than to Athens.

By providing educational opportunities for persons already licensed or ordained to the pastoral ministry, along with other key lay leaders, it is hoped that the real leaders in the church will be trained for ministry. Through growth in knowledge of Christ and the Scriptures, biblical theology and its interpretations, the development of skills for ministering, and through reflection upon one's actual practice of ministry, it is hoped that major strides will be taken in the development of the Christian ministry in Lancaster Mennonite Conference.

Educational Objectives

As pastors and students move through and complete the Mennonite Conference-Based Pastoral Education program it is hoped that they will:

1) grow in their faith commitment and knowledge of Christ and the life of obedient Christian discipleship;

2) gain knowledge of the Holy Scriptures, the centrality of Christ in divine revelation, the basic doctrines of the Christian faith, and the development of Christian theology in the history of the church;

3) understand more clearly and appreciate more deeply the saving gospel of Jesus Christ and learn how to communicate it to a modern world;

4) discover, appreciate, and incorporate the uniqueness of Anabaptist/Mennonite theology in their practice of ministry in today's world;

5) enhance their skills for ministry including preaching, administration, teaching, pastoral care, and evangelism;

6) develop their relational skills for the practice of ministry and for living in Christian community;

7) enable lay persons in the congregation to utilize their gifts for the larger mission of the church;

8) increase self-awareness in ministry by reflection upon their actual practice of ministry and work at increasing their competency through developing knowledge and skills for ministry;

9) relate and integrate actual experience of ministry in the congregation to learnings about the pastoral ministry;

10) grow in self-confidence as persons in ministry, develop appreciation for the pastoral calling, and grow in the enjoyment of the pastoral ministry.

The Mennonite Conference-Based Pastoral Education curriculum incorporates three major component parts: a Foundation Studies Program, Supervised Pastoral Education, and Continuing Education.

Foundation Studies Program

The Foundation Studies Program requires at least 60 credit hours of study. Any combination of two or three-hour Foundation

Studies courses making up the full 60 hours are needed to receive the Certificate in Pastoral Ministry. Courses are offered in two tracks so that students can arrange their schedule to fit the job setting in which they find themselves. At least six courses will be offered in each track of study each semester. The Evening Track consists of classes on Tuesday and Thursday evenings and Saturday mornings. Students may take a minimum of one course or a maximum of three courses per semester in this track. The Day Track likewise offers six courses of study Monday through Friday. Classes will be scheduled throughout the day so students can take a minimum of one course and a maximum of five courses per semester.

Each semester is fifteen weeks in length including examination week. The fall semester will normally run from early September to mid-December and the spring semester from early February to mid-May. In addition a special January term will offer several concentrated courses with classes every day, Monday through Friday, the first and second full weeks of January. Students may take only one course during this special January term. Normally, the spring and fall semesters offer three-hour courses and the January term offers two-hour courses. It is hoped that a special lectureship related to Anabaptist theology and/or the pastoral ministry, particularly preaching, can be established to accompany the January term.

Students can complete the Foundation Studies Program through the Day Track in two years and the Evening Track in four years. Total course offerings number 12 in Pastoral Theology (PT), 9 in Biblical Studies (BS), 5 in Theological Studies (ThS), 2 in Historical Studies (HS), 2 in English (Eng), and 1 in Sociology (Soc). Persons preparing for or actively involved in the pastoral ministry are required to take the following courses to receive the Foundation Studies Program Certificate.

Curriculum Outline

Year I, Semester I
Spiritual Formation and Spiritual Disciplines
Inductive Bible Study
Introduction to the New Testament
Pastoral Care and Counseling
Elective

January, Term I
Christian Discipleship and Ethics
Christian Peace and Justice

Year I, Semester II
Principles of Biblical Interpretation
Preaching in the Congregation
Old Testament History and Theology
Congregational Evangelism in the Believers' Church
Elective

Year II, Semester I
Introduction to New Testament Theology and Ethics
History of the Christian Church
Congregational Administration in the Believers' Church
The Context of Ministry
Elective

January, Term II
Preaching from Romans
The Gospel of Matthew

Year II, Semester II
Introduction to Theology
Mennonite History
Nurture in the Believers' Church
Anabaptist Theology
Elective

If students choose the Evening Track, the following courses should be taken.

Year I, Semester I
Spiritual Formation and Spiritual Disciplines
Inductive Bible Study

January Term
Christian Discipleship and Ethics

Year I, Semester II
Principles of Biblical Interpretation
Old Testament History and Theology

Year II, Semester I
Introduction to the New Testament
Pastoral Care and Counseling
Elective

January Term
Christian Peace and Justice

Year II, Semester II
Preaching in the Congregation
Congregational Evangelism in the Believers' Church
Elective

Year III, Semester I
Introduction to New Testament Theology and Ethics
History of the Christian Church
Elective

January Term
Preaching From Romans

Year III, Semester II
Introduction to Theology
Mennonite History
Elective

Year IV, Semester I
Congregational Administration in the Believers' Church
The Context of Ministry
Elective

January Term
The Gospel of Matthew

Year IV, Semester II
Anabaptist Theology
Nurture in the Believers' Church
Elective

The following are the descriptions of the required courses:

PT101. SPIRITUAL FORMATION AND THE SPIRITUAL DIS-CIPLINES

What must I be spiritually to lead a congregation? A course designed to develop the pastor's devotional life through experiences in the disciplines of Bible reading, prayer, fasting, reflection, and journaling. Various approaches to spiritual formation will be examined with a special focus on spiritual development from an Anabaptist/Mennonite perspective.

BS103. INDUCTIVE BIBLE STUDY

What does the biblical text say? By studying selected portions of Scripture students will observe firsthand major segments of thought, supporting themes, transition terms, etc. within the biblical text. Concentrating on the principles of observation, interpretation and application, students will be introduced to a basic inductive method of studying the Bible without the use of outside helps.

BS102. PRINCIPLES OF BIBLICAL INTERPRETATION

What does the biblical text mean? A study of the guiding principles in interpreting Scripture with the goal of understanding the meaning of Scripture for its first hearers and learning how to transfer its theological meaning to our world today. Grammatical, historical, theological and practical principles are considered along with Anabaptist hermeneutical insights.

PT201. THE CONTEXT OF MINISTRY

What is the social and cultural context in which I communicate the meaning of Scripture today? An analysis of the congregation, its cultural practices and the larger social and cultural framework in North America. A course designed to aid the student in learning how to contextualize the Christian message and work effectively with people in the congregation in carrying out the pastoral ministry.

PT104. PREACHING IN THE CONGREGATION

How do I communicate the meaning of Scripture in the context in which I minister? Basic principles of sermon construction and oral presentation with a special emphasis on effective communication of the biblical message. Students will discover the significance of preaching in the life of the church and work at preparing and delivering sermons.

BS105. OLD TESTAMENT HISTORY AND THEOLOGY

A basic introduction to the Old Testament noting how the Old Testament books arose. Primary attention will be given to God's revelation and Israel's faith response within history in contrast to other ancient Near Eastern peoples. Theological themes such as God, covenant, people of God, sin, salvation, worship, and the eschatological movement of thought in the Old Testament will also be studied.

BS106. INTRODUCTION TO THE NEW TESTAMENT

Beginning with the intertestamental period, this course will examine the political, social, religious, and economic world in which Christianity arose. Attention will be given to the sources of information on Christ and the early church, the historical development of the church, and the formation of the New Testament books.

BS203. INTRODUCTION TO NEW TESTAMENT THEOLOGY AND ETHICS

A study of the development of theology and ethics within the New Testament. Major themes examined include the kingdom of God, the person and work of Christ, understanding of the atonement and salvation, the nature and mission of the church, the person and work of the Holy Spirit, discipleship, eschatology, and the faithfulness and moral behavior of Christians.

HS205. HISTORY OF THE CHRISTIAN CHURCH

A study of the historical development of the church and its understanding of Christian theology as the church grew from its Mediterranean base to a worldwide body of Christ. Attention will be given to the patristic period and the early Christian creeds, the synthesis of church and state during the medieval period, renewal and development of the church through the Protestant Reformation, and the expansion and development of both eastern and western Christianity in the modern period.

HS204 MENNONITE HISTORY

A study of the origin and spread of sixteenth-century Anabaptism, martyrdom and development, migrations east and west in the seventeenth and eighteenth centuries, and the rapid growth of the Mennonite church through the missionary movement in third world countries. Special attention will be given to the role of the Mennonite Church in the history of the people of God.

ThS206. ANABAPTIST THEOLOGY

An in-depth study of the major theological themes in Anabaptist and Mennonite theology noting similarities and differences with other Christian theologies in the sixteenth and twentieth centuries. Attention will also be given to contributions Anabaptist theology can make to contemporary theological discussion.

ThS202. INTRODUCTION TO THEOLOGY
An introduction to the discipline of theology, the systematic method of doing theology, and major Christian doctrines as understood in systematic theology. This course will give an overview of the historic creeds of the Christian church and insights into various systems of theology with particular emphasis on the role of theology and ethics in the Mennonite Church.

PT107. PASTORAL CARE AND COUNSELING
A study of various approaches to pastoral care and the function of pastoral care in the total ministry. The place of worship, evangelism, nurture, visitation, and counseling in pastoral care will be noted. Attention will be given to developing counseling technique through a study of principles of pastoral counseling and introducing the student to kinds of pastoral counseling including crisis counseling, premarital and family counseling, vocational counseling, and financial counseling.

PT207. CONGREGATIONAL ADMINISTRATION IN THE BELIEVERS' CHURCH
Through a study of the theology and management of ministry this course introduces students to basic administrative principles for the congregation including discerning needs and developing mission statements, goal setting, organizing the congregation for mission, planning and implementing program, setting budgets, and evaluating progress.

PT108. CONGREGATIONAL EVANGELISM IN THE BELIEVERS' CHURCH
How does the congregation carry out its evangelistic witness in its setting? This course is designed to look at evangelistic theory and method by relating learnings to one's experience of evangelism in the congregation through supervision. Special attention will be given to the role of the pastor in equipping members for evangelism and service.

PT208. NURTURE IN THE BELIEVERS' CHURCH
How does the congregation nurture Christian believers for growth and mission? A study of the theoretical and practical elements of Christian education in the congregation from a believers' church perspective. Students will be supervised in teaching roles in the congregation.

In addition to the required courses, students may choose electives to complete credit hours needed to finish the Foundation Studies Program.

Eng101. WRITTEN COMMUNICATION
A basic college English composition course designed to teach the student English grammar and develop the student's ability to write with clarity, literary style, and expression.

Eng201. ORAL COMMUNICATION
A course designed to develop oral communication skills. Basic principles for preparing and delivering a speech will be noted. Students will be supervised in oral presentations through the use of video equipment, drama, and speeches given in the congregation.

PT104. WORSHIP IN THE BELIEVERS' CHURCH
A study of the significance of worship for God's people, how worship brings renewal through confession, affirmation of faith, and covenant renewal. The function of music, prayer, giving, and preaching in worship will be explored. Supervision will be given in worship planning including audience participation, balance between form and spontaneity, the use of visual aids, and learning how to lead people into God's presence.

PT206. MINISTRY TO THE FAMILY ·
A course designed to help pastors and family counselors work at family ministry. This course will review traits of the healthy family, discover how to help families identify their spiritual resources and analyze family systems. Supervision in family counseling will accompany the course including ways the pastor can help family members develop self-esteem, work at conflict resolution, and enhance family communication.

ThSJ109. CHRISTIAN DISCIPLESHIP AND ETHICS
A study of Jesus' call to follow him noting particularly the teachings of Jesus regarding kingdom ethics in the Sermon on the Mount. This course will also trace the early church's ethical teaching in relation to the person of Jesus. Students will explore the implications of discipleship and ethics when applied to vocations represented in the congregation such as medicine, education, business, law, manufacturing and sales, clerking, farming, and the arts.

ThSJ110. CHRISTIAN PEACE AND JUSTICE

In this course students will be introduced to the biblical teaching on peacemaking and the call to social and economic justice. The course will explore the worldwide church and its implications for peacemaking in the contemporary world. The church's relation to the political order will be examined from New Testament and Anabaptist perspectives.

PTJ210. PREACHING FROM ROMANS

A study of the book of Romans and the use of its major theological themes in preaching. This course will consider the underlying argument of the book, its significance in the formation of Christian doctrine, and how the student can do relevant biblical preaching from its contents.

BSJ209. THE GOSPEL OF MATTHEW

An inductive study of Matthew's gospel noting its underlying structure, central theme and interpretation of the new kingdom of God for the Jewish community. Special attention will be given to holy history and the place of Jesus in fulfilling the Old Testament, the Sermon on the Mount, and Jesus's teaching regarding the kingdom of God.

BS205. THE EPISTLE TO THE HEBREWS

A study of the uniqueness of Jesus in comparison to the major Old Testament offices of prophet, priest, and king. Special attention will be given to the nature of the atonement and the formation of the New Covenant in Jesus Christ.

BS108. THE GOSPEL OF JOHN

An inductive study of the fourth gospel noting the profoundness of Jesus's teaching regarding life, belief, love, and obedience. The underlying nature of belief and unbelief will be noted as well as the uniqueness of the upper room discourse.

BS202. THE BOOK OF REVELATION

In the midst of twentieth century pop eschatology, the student in this course will be introduced to an in-depth study of this tract for hard times noting especially the nature of apocalyptic literature, the victory of Christ and the church, and the nature of the Christian hope.

PT212. MASS MEDIA AND THE CHRISTIAN MINISTRY

An analysis of the effect of mass media upon people's value system and its effect on the church. The course will also examine the positive and negative implications of religious broadcasting. Several contemporary religious television programs will be analyzed to discern their theology as well as strengths and weaknesses in communicating the Christian message.

ThSJ208. TWENTIETH CENTURY THEOLOGY

A survey of the background and development of major theological movements in the twentieth century including fundamentalism, liberalism, neo-orthodoxy, evangelicalism, secular theology, liberation theology, and charismatic theology.

PT105. LAY COUNSELING IN THE BELIEVERS' CHURCH

A course designed to mobilize lay persons for the counseling ministry by learning basic principles of counseling, developing listening skills, learning how to write and reflect on verbatims, and knowing when to make referrals.

SOC205. URBAN SOCIOLOGY

An investigation into the nature of life in the urban community with special attention given to forces affecting the conflicts between inner city, middle city, outer city, and suburbia. Also the student will be introduced to various cultural groups and how culture affects the church. The class will look at major social ills of the day and ways the church can respond to these needs.

In order to enhance the learning process teachers will be asked to prepare study guides for the students as aids for preparing each class session. To enhance the education retention process and identify issues for further study, students are required to keep a journal for each course. These journals are to reflect the students' work outside of class on a weekly basis and become the source for class discussion. Four columns of information comprise these journals: learnings from experience in ministry, learnings from outside readings or other assignments, class notes and questions for further study due to integrating experience, outside reading, and class notes.

Supervised Pastoral Education

The second component of Mennonite Conference-Based Pastoral Education is Supervised Pastoral Education. In order to provide a supervised program for bivocational pastors, many of whom have not completed seminary or college, a modified parish-based program is suggested. In this program six active pastors are recruited to meet with a supervisor one day per week for seventeen weeks. Each pastor prepares and presents several acts of ministry for supervision through case conferences and individual supervision. All material presented in the case conference and individual supervisory hour grows out of the actual pastoral ministry of the persons enrolled in the program. Thus the action/reflection educational method is used.

In this program the living human document is the congregation itself with supervision focusing not only on how the pastor goes about his/her acts of ministry, but also on how the pastor relates to peers and to the living human document in the process of pastoral ministry. Teaching seminars call the pastor's attention to various aspects of the pastoral ministry as well as human growth and development of individuals in the congregation. An interpersonal relations hour enables the six pastors to observe their relational skills by receiving feedback from peers and sharing personal concerns with one another.

Unlike hospital-based CPE, the modified Supervised Pastoral Education Program focuses on the role of the pastor in *developing the life of the congregation as the living human document* rather than restricting one's ministry to persons in crisis and focusing on pathology. Case conferences review preaching acts of ministry, administrative acts of ministry, pastoral care and counseling acts of ministry, hospital calling, evangelistic efforts, etc.

This modified Supervised Pastoral Education Program emerges from research in experience-based learning and my own experience of working with Paul M. Miller, CPE supervisor, since 1982 in supervised education for pastors in Lancaster Mennonite Conference. The following course syllabus reflects my current thinking on this component of pastoral education.

THE SUPERVISED PASTORAL EDUCATION PROGRAM
OF LANCASTER MENNONITE CONFERENCE
September 1986 - December 1986

1. Objectives
The program offers to selected pastors in the Lancaster Mennonite Conference area the opportunity to receive supervision of portions of the pastoral ministry in which they are presently engaged. Although the program will not seek accreditation with the American

Association of Clinical Pastoral Education, the program shall adhere closely to the standards of one-half unit of Basic CPE. It is important that a "contact person" be secured from every congregation in which a supervised pastor is serving so that immediate feedback is possible. The contact person shall cooperate with the supervisee and the supervisor so that the best interests of the congregation are protected and served.

2. Administration

The Leadership Council of Lancaster Mennonite Conference is responsible for the program of Supervised Pastoral Education in the area it represents. It shall approve programs, budgets, publicity, and financing of the program. Paul M. Zehr is staff person of the Leadership Council.

3. Essential Elements of the Program

    a. a specific time period (17 weeks each term);
    b. twelve hours on duty each week as a pastor in his/her own congregation;
    c. one full day each week of reporting and evaluation of that ministry;
    d. peer group assistance and evaluation in ministry (weekly);
    e. individual supervision, every other week, with the SPE supervisor;
    f. participation in an interpersonal relations group of peers;
    g. theological integration and reflection throughout the program;
    h. an individual contract for learning and growth in ministry.

4. Goal for the Program

During 1986 the program offered Supervised Pastoral Education to six pastors in the Lancaster Mennonite Conference area. The seventeen-week program began Friday, August 29, 1986 and met every Friday through December 19, 1986.

5. Resource Persons Available for the Program

Selected resource persons assisted in the program. Dr. Paul M. Zehr, Dr. Enos D. Martin, and Dr. Paul M. Miller were the main resource persons. Additional resource persons were invited to assist from mental health institutions, CPE Centers in the area as well as conference and church leaders active in the helping professions.

6. **Admission to the Program**
    Applicants interested in the program were interviewed by Dr. Paul M. Miller, CPE Supervisor and Director of the program. They were endorsed by their bishop or overseer and approved by their congregation for the program. The Leadership Council may invite selected pastors to consider participating, bishops may recommend pastors, congregations may initiate, and individual pastors may request admission, but, in any case, all parties listed above must give their approval.

7. **Expectations and Requirements of the SPE Student**
    a. twelve hours of pastoral services in the congregation each week;
    b. not more than one absence (unexcused) from Supervisory Day;
    c. two reading reports of books read (approved by Supervisor);
    d. eight verbatim reports of acts of ministry (tape recordings, etc.); these must include one "critical incident" report or one "proposal" or "position paper" on an issue crucial in the congregation;
    e. written midterm evaluation, due the eighth week of the program;
    f. final self-evaluation, due the seventeenth week.

8. **Schedule for the Weekly Supervisory Day**
    8:00 - 8:30 Devotional Period and "Spiritual Formation Concerns"
    8:30 - 9:30 Case Conference
    9:30 - 10:30 Interpersonal Relations Hour
    10:30 - 11:00 Break
    11:00 - 12:15 Teaching Seminar
    12:15 - 1:00 Lunch
    1:00 - 2:00 Case Conference
    2:00 - 3:00 Individual Supervision
    3:00 - 4:00 Individual Supervision

9. **Transcript Credit Awarded**
    Students enrolled in the Supervised Pastoral Education Program are eligible to receive four hours of credit from Eastern Mennonite Seminary. In order to receive that credit they must register for it.

10. **Cost**
    The cost for students was $1,000 of which $200 was normally

paid personally by the student. The participating congregations paid
$800; additional subsidy was provided by the Lancaster Mennonite
Conference. In some cases congregations paid the total $1,000 for
their pastor.

Continuing Education

The third and final component of Mennonite Conference-
Based Pastoral Education is continuing education. Learning continues throughout life. Pastors learn year after year through the
practice of ministry. There is a tendency, however, to experience
staleness in preaching unless one feeds his/her mind and spirit
through continuing education. Some pastors experience burnout as
a result of constantly pouring out their knowledge and self in ministry while neglecting to feed their mind and spirit on new material.

A continuing education program is designed to meet these
needs as part of a larger pastoral training program. Since 1980
classes of this nature have been offered with enrollment as high as
fifty persons. Two classes per year are proposed, one in the fall and
the other in the spring, for pastors and key lay leaders in the congregations. These classes are offered on ten consecutive Thursday
evenings so persons can give one night per week to continuing
education. During the spring term a seminary teacher is engaged as
Scholar-in-Residence to teach a subject of current interest to
pastors. This exchange with the seminary brings to the district conference the best in pastoral and theological education and at the
same time helps the seminary keep in touch with the congregations
of the denomination in the Lancaster area.

Course selections are determined by the director of pastoral
training for Lancaster Mennonite Conference in consultation with
the directors of pastoral training from the Atlantic Coast Mennonite
Conference and the Franconia Mennonite Conference. The three
directors report to an Interconference Pastoral Training Program
Board made up of representatives from the three Mennonite district
conferences in southeastern Pennsylvania. Experience over the past
five years indicates attendance in these classes, which are now
identified as Continuing Education classes, runs as high as fifty or
more pastors and lay leaders from Lancaster Mennonite Conference. These Continuing Education classes for bishops, ministers,
deacons, and key lay leaders can continue throughout the years of
ministry. Directors need to determine what classes to offer both on
the basis of contemporary needs and on the basis of providing a
balanced continuing education program for congregational leaders.

The following syllabus is an example of one of these courses which was offered in Spring, 1984.

Themes in Old Testament Theology
Paul M. Zehr, Coordinator

I. Course description
An introduction to major theological themes in the Old Testament. Special attention will be given to Israel's understanding of Yahweh through divine revelation and the nature of Israel's peoplehood within the call to covenant community.

II. Course Objectives
A. To understand the revelation of God to Israel;
B. to discern and appreciate the meaning for covenant community and the significance of the people of God within God's redemptive purpose in history;
C. to comprehend the movement of God in Israel's history toward Jesus Christ and its implications for relating the Testaments to each other.

III. Course Procedure
Several persons will lecture on the basic themes in Old Testament theology. Class participants shall read widely and enter into discussion of the themes.

IV. Texts
Anderson, B. W. *Understanding the Old Testament.* Third edition. Englewood Cliffs, N.J.: Prentice-Hall, Inc., 1975.
Hasel, G. *Old Testament Theology: Basic Issues in the Current Debate.* Revised edition. Grand Rapids: William B. Eerdmans Publishing Company, 1975.
Martens, E. *God's Design: A Focus on Old Testament Theology.* Grand Rapids: Baker Book House, 1981.

V. Course Requirements for Credit
A. Read Hasel's book and one of the other texts;
B. read 500 pages from books listed in the bibliography;

C.   prepare a research paper (6 to 8 pages) on a theological theme in the Old Testament (paper topic must be approved by the coordinator);

D.   enter into discussion and take notes from class lectures.

VI.   Course Themes
   A.   Prolegomena - Genesis 1-11   (Paul M. Zehr)
   B.   The Exodus-Sinai Events   (Paul M. Zehr)
        - Yahweh's Revelation
        - Redemption from Egypt
   C.   The Exodus-Sinai Events   (Paul M. Zehr)
        - Formation of a Covenant Community
        - Law and Worship
   D.   Monotheism and its Adversaries   (Paul M. Zehr)
        - Worldly Politics, Baalism, Wealth, Worship
   E.   The Prophetic Word: Amos and Hosea(Thomas F. McDaniel)
        - The Breakdown of Covenant Community
        - Call to Covenant Renewal
   F.   The Prophetic Word: Isaiah and Micah(Thomas F. McDaniel)
        - Judgment and Restoration
   G.   The Prophetic Word: Jeremiah and Ezekiel   (Thomas F. McDaniel)
        - The Crisis of the Exile
        - Promise of a New Covenant
   H.   The Praises of Israel   (Bernhard W. Anderson)
   I.   From the Prophetic Message to the Apocalyptic Message   (Ben C. Ollenburger)
   J.   The Relationship Between the Testaments (Paul M. Zehr)
        - Promise and Fulfillment

These three components--Foundation Studies Program, Supervised Pastoral Education, and Continuing Education--comprise the curriculum guide for Mennonite Conference-Based Pastoral Education of Lancaster Mennonite Conference.

ENDNOTES

1. Richard C. Detweiler, "Summary of Pastoral Survey in Nine Conferences of Region V and the Conservative Conference of the Mennonite Church", an unpublished paper in the writer's files, 1981. See also Marlin E. Miller and Marcus Smucker, "A Summary of Findings From the Ministerial/Leadership Survey," an unpublished paper in the writer's files, 1981.

2. Markus Barth, *Ephesians: Introduction, Translation and Commentary*. Vols. 1-2 (Garden City, NY: Doubleday, 1974), 479.

3. J. F. Hopewell, "A Congregational Paradigm for Theological Education," *Theological Education* 21 (I), 60.

4. Edward Farley, "Can Church Education be Theological Education?" *Theology Today* 42 (2), 158-171.

5. Avery Dulles, *Models of the Church* (Garden City, NY: Doubleday, 1974), 165.

6. *Ibid.*, 67-69.

7. Daniel Hertzler, *Mennonite Education: Why and How? A Philosophy of Education for the Mennonite Church* (Scottdale, PA: Herald Press, 1971).

8. Ross T. Bender, *The People of God: A Mennonite Interpretation of the Free Church Tradition* (Scottdale, PA: Herald Press, 1971).

9. C. J. Dyck, "Anabaptist-Mennonite Perspectives," in Leland Harder, editor, *Perspectives on the Nurturing of Faith* (Elkhart, IN: Institute of Mennonite Studies, 1983), 136.

10. Paton Yoder, "Toward a Mennonite Philosophy of Education Since 1890," an unpublished paper presented at the Philosophy of Christian Education Study Workshop for the Mennonite Church, September 13-16, 1968, 18.

11. J. Lawrence Burkholder, "Theological Education for the Believers' Church," *Concern* 17 (February 1969), 10-11.

12. Farley, "Can Church Education ...?" 166-167.

13. Bender, *The People of God*, 166.

14. K. B. Mulholland, *Adventures in Training the Ministry* (Philadelphia: Presbyterian and Reformed Publishing Company, 1976), 79.

15. F. Ross Kinsler, "Open Theological Education," *Theological Education* 10 (Winter 1974), 235.

16. F. Ross Kinsler, *Ministry by the People: Theological Education by Extension* (Maryknoll, NY: Orbis, 1983), 15-16.

17. David Kornfeld, "Seminary Education: Toward Adult Education Alternatives," in *Missions and Theological Education in World Perspective*, H. M. Conn and S. F. Rowen, editors (Farmington, MI: Associates of Urbanus, 1984), 198.

18. R. R. Covell and C. Peter Wagner, *An Extension Seminary Primer* (Pasadena, CA: William Carey Library, 1971), 39-40.

19. C. Peter Wagner, "Seminaries Ought to be Asking Who as Well as How," in *Theological Education* 10 (Summer 1974), 269.

20. Kornfeld, *Seminary Education*, 197.

21. Mulholland, *Adventures*, 66.

22. E. E. Thornton, *Professional Education for Ministry* (Nashville: Abingdon, 1970), 74-110.

23. *Ibid.*, 111-196; 250-264.

24. R. C. Powell, *CPE: Fifty Years of Learning Through Supervised Encounter With Living Human Documents* (New York: The Association for Clinical Pastoral Education, Inc., 1975), 207.

25. R. E. Thompson, "Parish-based Supervised Pastoral Education at Northlea United Church, Toronto, Ontario," D. Min. Dissertation at the University of Toronto, 1985, 14.

26. J. Y. Hammett, "A Social Drink at the Well: Theological and Philosophical Context of CPE Origins," *The Journal of Pastoral Care* 29 (2), 88.

27. *Ibid.*, 89.

28. Don S. Browning, *The Moral Context of Pastoral Care* (Philadelphia: Westminster, 1976), 15.

29. Thornton, *Professional Education for Ministry*, 167-168.

30. William H. Willimon, *Worship as Pastoral Care* (Nashville: Abingdon, 1979), 38.

31. Robert K. Nace, "Parish Clinical Pastoral Education: Redefining the 'Living Human Document,'" *The Journal of Pastoral Care* 35 (March 1981), 59.

32. *Ibid.*, 59-60.

33. Archie MacLachlan, cited in Thompson, "Parish-based Supervised Pastoral Education," 99.

34. Bender, *The People of God*, 166.

35. *Ibid.*, 166.

36. Walter Klaassen, *Anabaptism: Neither Catholic Nor Protestant* (Waterloo, Ontario: Conrad Press, 1973), 20-21; see also Irvin B. Horst, "The Role of Christian Education in the Churches of the Anabaptist Tradition," in *The Witness of the Holy Spirit: Proceedings of the Eighth Mennonite World Conference* (Elkhart, IN: 1967), 216.

BIBLIOGRAPHY

Barth, Markus. *Ephesians: Introduction, Translation and Commentary.* 2 vols. Garden City, NY: Doubleday and Co., 1974.

Bender, Ross T. *The People of God: A Mennonite Interpretation of the Free Church Tradition.* Scottdale, PA: Herald Press, 1971.

Browning, Don S. *The Moral Context of Pastoral Care.* Philadelphia: The Westminster Press, 1976.

Burkholder, J. Lawrence. "Theological Education in the Believers' Church." *Concern* 17 (1969): 10-32.

Covell R. R. and Wagner, C. Peter. *An Extension Seminary Primer.* South Pasadena, CA: William Carey Library, 1971.

Detweiler, Richard C. "Summary of Pastoral Survey in Nine Conferences of Region V and the Conservative Conference of the Mennonite Church." Unpublished paper in the writer's files, 1981.

Dulles, Avery. *Models of the Church.* Garden City, NY: Doubleday and Co., Inc., 1974.

Dyck, C. J. "Anabaptist-Mennonite Perspectives." In *Perspectives on the Nurturing of Faith,* edited by Leland Harder, 132-151. Elkhart, IN: Institute of Mennonite Studies, 1983.

Farley, Edward. "Can Church Education be Theological Education?" *Theology Today* 42 (July 1985): 158-171.

Hammett, J. Y. "A Social Drink at the Well: Theological and Philosophical Context of CPE Origins." *The Journal of Pastoral Care* 29 (1079): 86-89.

Hopewell, J. F. "A Congregational Paradigm for Theological Education." *Theological Education* 21 (Autumn 1984): 60-70.

Hertzler, Daniel. *Mennonite Education: Why and How? A Philosophy of Education for the Mennonite Church.* Scottdale, PA: Herald Press, 1971.

Horst, Irvin B. "The Role of Christian Education in the Churches of the Anabaptist Tradition." In *The Witness of the Holy Spirit*. Proceedings of the Eighth Mennonite World Conference. Elkhart, IN (1967): 208-17.

Kinsler, F. Ross. *Ministry by the People*. Maryknoll, NY: Orbis Books, 1983.

Kinsler, F. Ross. "Open Theological Education." *Theological Education* 10 (1974), 234-245.

Klaassen, Walter. *Anabaptism: Neither Catholic Nor Protestant*. Waterloo, Ontario: Conrad Press, 1973.

Kornfeld, D. "Seminary Education: Toward Adult Education Alternatives." In *Missions and Theological Education in World Perspective*, edited by H. M. Conn and S. F. Rowen, 169-225. Farmington, MI: Associates of Urbanus, 1984.

Miller, Marlin E. and Smucker, Marcus G. "A Summary of Findings From the Ministerial/Leadership Survey." Unpublished paper in the writer's files, 1981.

Mulholland, K. B. *Adventures in Training the Ministry*. Philadelphia: Presbyterian and Reformed Publishing Company, 1976.

Nace, R. K. "Parish Clinical Pastoral Education: Redefining 'the Living Human Document.'" *The Journal of Pastoral Care* 35 (March 1981), 58-68.

Powell, R. C. *CPE: Fifty Years of Learning Through Supervised Encounter with Living Human Documents*. New York: The Association for Clinical Pastoral Education, Inc., 1975.

Thompson, R. E. "Parish-based Supervised Pastoral Education at Northlea United Church, Toronto, Ontario. "Unpublished Doctor of Ministry Dissertation, Victoria University and the University of Toronto, 1985.

Thornton, E. E. *Professional Education for Ministry*. Nashville: Abingdon Press, 1970.

Wagner, C. Peter. "Seminaries Ought to be Asking Who as Well as How." *Theological Education* 10 (1974), 266-274.

Willimon, William H. *Worship as Pastoral Care*. Nashville: Abingdon, 1979.

Yoder, Paton. "Toward a Mennonite Philosophy of Education Since 1980." Unpublished paper presented at Philosophy of Christian Education Study Workshop for the Mennonite Church, September 13-16, 1968.

Chapter 2

Leadership Training for the Church of the Future

Jim Egli

1. The Purpose of this Study

When I was nineteen years old, I was living with my parents while majoring in business at a local junior college. That fall my pastor, Mahlon Miller, invited me to join two others whom he was training in a Pastoral Apprentice Program. This class involved teaching sessions, plenty of reading, and practical ministry opportunities. It was my first experience in pastoral training and was a turning point in my life as my own call to ministry emerged through the prayer, support, and counsel of this group. That program also planted a seed within, an interest in the methods of pastoral education.

Since then, I have been involved in many forms of ministerial training, both as a student and a teacher. Besides studying in the classroom, I've gotten credit for digging wells and preaching in the jungle of Costa Rica. I've taken correspondence courses and also studied in the tutorial system of Oxford University.

Later as a Bible teacher in Africa from 1980 to 1983, I worked with Theological Education by Extension and other decentralized approaches to train African pastors in the countries of Lesotho and the Transkei. Since then I have completed my master's thesis on the call and training of Mennonite pastors, co-authored a leadership training manual, and organize presently an annual pastoral training event. Through all of this my interest and research on the equipping of pastoral leaders have grown. Many questions have been turning in my mind. How do persons receive a call to leadership ministry? How are pastors and other leaders best trained? What are the key biblical examples and principles? What are the strengths and disadvantages of the various training approaches?

In all my experiences and research my questions have focused more on methods than on content. For many years our schools and churches have been concerned with content: "*What* should we teach potential pastors?" The question, "*How* should we teach them?" has not received as much attention, at least, not until recently. This treatise explores the "how" of leadership training.

I begin this study with the biblical material looking in the first two chapters at the leadership training methods of Jesus and then

Paul. The following chapter looks at the Mennonite church, reviewing developments in our churches from the time of the Anabaptists until now. After that I turn to the experience of present pastors, reporting the results of my field research among Mennonite pastors of Illinois. Finally, I explore the current rethinking of pastoral training that is taking place around the world.

In studying pastoral training from these biblical, historical, experiential, and educational perspectives, I have concluded that effective leadership training is not primarily a matter of acquiring information and learning to think theologically. It is much more a matter of learning how to relate -- growing in our relationship with and dependence on God and learning how to love and minister to others. This growth in relationships and relational skills involves several crucial elements: a deep reliance on God through prayer, an apprentice relationship with a local pastor or leader, the support of other believers, cognitive learning, and actual involvement in ministry. In order to be dynamically effective these elements must be intertwined with each other at each point in the equipping process.

The research and conclusions given here are a reworking and condensing of my master's thesis at Lincoln Christian Seminary, Lincoln, Illinois. I am grateful to that seminary for their permission to reproduce much of that thesis in this present form.

2. Leadership Training Jesus' Style

How did Jesus equip leaders? Why was his leadership training so effective? How did he transform a motley crew of disciples into dynamic witnesses? What can we learn from Christ's example for our present task of leadership development?

Even a casual study of Jesus' leadership training should jar the twentieth century church because the priority he gave this equipping ministry and the methods he used differ markedly from our own. Training leaders was of supreme importance to Christ.

He brought his group of trainees into an intense relationship with himself where he modeled prayer and ministry, taught them, interacted with them, and then involved them and supervised them in actual ministry. This in-service training did more than confer information and skills, it imparted Jesus' lifestyle and values. Various key principles emerge in the Gospels from Jesus' example which we must seek to apply in our ministries and churches today.

Jesus Gave Leadership Training Top Priority

Jesus devoted a startling amount of time to leadership training.[1] This is clear in the Gospels, especially in Mark. Of the 550 verses in Mark which record Jesus' overall ministry, 282 show Jesus relating to the public, and 268 show him working more closely with his twelve trainees.[2] Illustrated it looks like this:

Jesus' Ministry in Mark

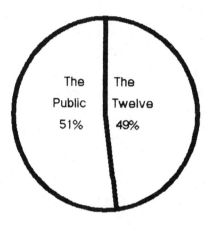

The Public 51%

The Twelve 49%

    This reveals that leadership training was central to Jesus' ministry and required an astounding amount of time. Yet Jesus gave it this priority because he saw it as a primary ingredient in expanding God's kingdom. My statistics substantiate the claim of A. B. Bruce that the training of the disciples was Jesus' top concern:

> Both from His words and from His actions we can see that He attached supreme importance to that part of His work which consisted in training the twelve. In the intercessory prayer, (John 17:6), *e.g.*, He speaks of the training He had given these men as if it had been the principle part of His own earthly ministry. And such, in one sense, it really was. The careful, painstaking education of the disciples secured that the Teacher's influence on the world should be permanent; that His kingdom should be founded on the rock of deep and indestructible convictions in the minds of the few, not on the shifting sands of superficial evanescent impressions on the minds of the many.[3]

    As this quote hints, Jesus' prayers reflect the centrality of leadership training in his ministry. We get only glimpses into Jesus' prayer life in the Gospels, yet so much of what we see shows him praying for his disciples. Jesus' night of prayer (Luke 6:12-16), the "High Priestly" prayer (John 17:6-18), and the prayer for failing Simon (Luke 22:31), all show us Christ at prayer for this core group of potential leaders.

Jesus' ministry had focus. His goal was to reach the world, but his method for accomplishing this was to equip a handful of leaders who could multiply his own effort. So Jesus poured his life - his time, his efforts, his prayers - into this intimate group of followers.

Training the disciples was frustrating and time consuming, but it paid off. After Jesus' brief ministry of several years, the future of the church depended on these leaders. When the gospel exploded on the scene of the Roman Empire, it sprang more from the Spirit-empowered witness of these intimate followers than from the general populace which thronged Christ's ministry.

Jesus Trained Leaders at Different Levels

To pattern our leadership training after Jesus we pastors and other leaders should be working at equipping ministry on different levels at the same time. Jesus' ministry as presented in Mark shows us three spheres of influence which can be illustrated like this:

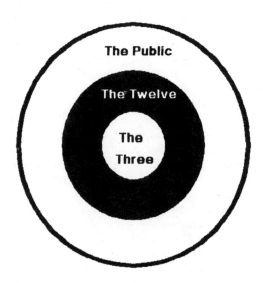

First, there is the public sphere. Jesus demonstrated and expressed a definite call to public ministry; throughout the Gospels we see him serving and interacting with the general populace.

Within this sphere is another, The Twelve. Jesus chose twelve special followers (3:13ff). He poured his time and effort into this group and fought the pressures of the crowds so that he could train them (9:30-31).

Then within this group of twelve, Jesus worked even more closely with a select group of The Three - Peter, James, and John (5:37ff; 9:2ff; 13:3ff; 14:33ff). The importance of this smaller group is emphasized by the prominent place given to their initial calling (1:16ff) and the listing of their names at the very beginning of the roll of disciples (3:16f).

The sections of Mark's Gospel where Jesus interacts with these three contain 82 verses. This is 31 percent of the 268 verses related to the disciples or 15 percent of Jesus' overall ministry. These segments include such important events as Christ's transfiguration and his intense prayer in Gethsemane.

Noting this further concentration of Jesus on The Three, Robert Coleman observes:

> All of this certainly impresses one with the deliberate way that Jesus proportioned His life to those He wanted to train. It also graphically illustrates a fundamental principle of teaching: that other things being equal, the more concentrated the size of the group being taught, the greater the opportunity for effective instruction.[4]

Jesus' example challenges and illuminates our own leadership training. We haven't given this equipping of leaders on different levels anything approaching the priority Christ placed on it. Could it be that his example is normative? Could it be that such deliberate discipling and training, as time consuming and frustrating as it may be, is the key to unleashing the gospel?

Jesus Brought His Learners into a Deep Relationship with Himself

Jesus invited learners into a relationship of intense interaction and sharing as he charged them, "Come, follow me" (Mark 1:17; Matt. 9:9; John 1:43). Through the years of his ministry they would eat together, pray together, minister together, and travel together. Mark, in fact, emphasizes that the primary role of the Twelve was "that they might be *with* him" (3:14). That the foundational aspect of Jesus' training approach was its relational character should not surprise us. Modern educational theory emphasizes that a positive instructor-learner relationship itself is the most powerful tool for teaching, influencing, motivating. Jesus' training of the Twelve was relationship centered rather than program or content centered.

Because the disciples were literally bound to follow Jesus, they observed him in the many diverse situations of daily life and ministry. They not only learned skills and heard his teaching, they also caught his lifestyle. In this context, sayings such as this one from Mark 10:43-45 took on depth and clarity:

> Whoever wants to become great among you must be your servant, and whoever wants to be first must be the slave of all. For even the Son of Man did not come to be served, but to serve, and to give his life as a ransom for many.

This close association of Jesus with the disciples also let him personalize his training, responding to the specific needs, strengths and weaknesses of each individual.

Jesus Taught by Demonstration

Seldom do we see Jesus by himself in the Gospels. When he preached, healed, taught, debated opponents, or delivered demoniacs, he was almost always accompanied by his disciples. In this way, Jesus was constantly modeling ministry skills and teaching by demonstration. The disciples learned by observation and could later ask Jesus follow-up questions during more relaxed moments (e.g., Mark 4:10; 9:28).

Jesus did not merely *tell* the disciples how to live, he actually *showed* them how to pray, preach, teach and share. Robert Munger has described the impact this must have had on the disciples:

> Jesus did not establish a school of discipleship in a local synagogue. He called twelve to be with Him in a form of 'in-service' training. The disciples not only heard Him teach but observed what He did and how He did it. They saw His response to the sick, the lame, the blind, and the hungry. They would never forget how He touched a leper, forgave a sinful woman, and received a social outcast. They caught His compassion for the multitude and heard Him sob over Jerusalem. They would remember His anger over the defilement of the Temple and the way He parried the thrusts of His adversaries. In His responses to people and situations they caught His attitudes as well as His act. Living with Him day and night, they received a model of the way life is to be lived and their own lives were indelibly marked. They would remember and try to repeat in their own ministry what they had seen in Him. [5]

Jesus Involved His Learners in Actual Ministry

From the very beginning Jesus chose his disciples for the purpose of ministry: "He appointed twelve. . . that he might send them out to preach and to have authority to drive out demons" (Mark 3:14). The disciples' involvement in ministry is seen clearly in the preaching and healing mission on which Jesus sent them in pairs in Mark 6:7-13. Notice the debriefing which seems to have followed this experience in the ongoing training process (Mark 6:30-31).

Apparently, Jesus sent the Twelve on several such campaigns. In Mark 9:14-29, some of the disciples are again ministering on their own; this time the result is an unsuccessful attempt to free a boy of demon possession (vv. 14-19). When Jesus comes upon the situation and brings deliverance to the child (vv. 20-27), this becomes an occasion for questions and instruction (vv. 28-29). There are tremendous advantages in placing training in the context of actual ministry: motivation to learn is high, questions are completely relevant, teaching is directly and immediately applied, individual guidance and supervision are possible.

By training leaders through demonstration and involvement in real ministry, Jesus was giving his disciples the very skills they would later need for service and leadership on their own. This is where our present training systems often fail miserably. By relying on an academic model, we require students to acquire a special set of skills, but these skills are different from those actually needed in the work of ministry. In leadership training the method is the message because learners assume both consciously and unconsciously that the skills we ask them to learn are the same ones they will later need. Jesus' leadership training was dynamic and effective because it taught the precise skills, attitudes, and information that his disciples would use in their own ministries.

Jesus Modeled and Taught a Life of Prayer

Jesus placed a high priority on teaching his disciples to pray. In the same way that Jesus' ongoing sense of call emerged out of his experience of prayer (Mark 1:35ff; John 5:19), so the disciples' urge to preach and ability to minister would proceed from their own life of prayer. Jesus taught that prayer preceded action (Matt. 10:37ff; Mark 9:28f).

On this teaching of prayer, A. B. Bruce has said:

It would have been matter for surprise if, among the manifold subjects on which Jesus gave instruction to His disciples, prayer had not occupied a prominent place. Prayer is a necessity of spiritual life, and all who earnestly try to pray soon feel the need of teaching on how to do it. And what theme more likely to engage the thoughts of a Master who was Himself emphatically a man of prayer, spending occasionally whole nights in prayerful communion with His heavenly Father (Mark 1:35; Luke 6:12; Matt. 14:23)?[6]

Besides modeling a life of prayer, Jesus also gave a lot of specific instruction to the disciples on how to pray (e.g. Matt. 5:44; 6:5ff; Mark 11:20ff; Luke 11:1ff; 18:9ff). In Acts, we discover that this priority of prayer carried into the life of the early church under the direction of the apostles (1:14; 2:42; 4:24; 12:5; 13:1ff). The word "Abba" in the prayer life of the early Christians (Rom 8:15; Gal 4:6) suggests that they captured the intimacy and spontaneity of Jesus' relationship to God through prayer.

This centrality of prayer in Jesus' leadership training challenges our approach which essentially places academics - the cognitive and intellectual - at the core. Just as prayer was crucial to Jesus' ministry, so he taught that it must be for the disciples. The effectiveness of our own training methods can be measured by their ability to instill a life of prayer.

Jesus Rejected the Established Educational Pattern

Even though Jesus is called "Rabbi" in the Gospels by both his followers (Mark 11:21; 14:45) and others (Mark 10:51; John 3:2), his training methods differed radically from the Rabbinic system.[7] Jesus freely rejected the established training model and used a pattern specifically geared to his own goals. It is important for us to see the differences between Jesus' methods and the Rabbinic ones for two reasons: first, to understand the genius of Jesus' effectiveness; and secondly, to become aware that the pattern Jesus rejected looks surprisingly like the academic, residential model we have embraced today.

Jesus' call to discipleship was a call to service. In Mark 1:17 and Luke 5:10 the call is to be fishers of men. When the Twelve were sent out, their assignment was to proclaim God's kingdom, to heal, and to cast out demons (Matt. 10:4,8). Such action was not the goal in the Rabbinic schools where the emphasis was on study and learning[8] (Rengstorf 2:142), with the student himself one day becoming a Rabbi in an ongoing chain of tradition (Rengstorf 4:454). Jesus adamantly rejected this system (Matt. 23:5-10).[9]

Of course, Jesus' teaching contained cognitive elements as his discourses and parables demonstrate, yet his essential call was to service, not academic or informational learning. In fact, T. W. Manson, in his book *The Teaching of Jesus,* has suggested that the original Aramaic word behind disciple (Greek *mathetes*) was not *talmida*, whose Hebrew equivalent talmid was used for the Rabbinic disciples. He argues convincingly that the more probable word was *showli*. If this is true, we should take mathetes to mean "apprentice" rather than "student" as it sometimes does in other Koine Greek usage.[10] Manson goes on to discuss what the implications of this could be:

> Why *showli* rather than *talmida* as our Lord's designation of his disciples?
>
> It is tempting to see in the choice of the word a definite opposition to the whole scribal system. The *talmid* of the Rabbinical schools is primarily a student. His chief business was to master the contents of the written Law and the oral Tradition. The finished products of the Rabbinical schools were learned biblical scholars and sound and competent lawyers. The life of a *talmid* as *talmid* was made up of study of the sacred writings, attendance of lectures, and discussion of difficult passages or cases. Discipleship as Jesus conceived it was not a theoretical discipline of this sort, but a practical task to which men were called to give themselves and all their energies. Their work was not study but practice. Fishermen were to become fishers of men, peasants were to be labourers in God's vineyard or God's harvest field. And Jesus was their Master not so much as a teacher of right doctrine, but rather as the master-craftsman whom they were to follow and imitate. Discipleship was not matriculation in a Rabbinical College but apprenticeship to the work of the Kingdom. It may be added that there is something appropriate in the choice of 'apprentices' rather than 'students' as the name for the disciples of Jesus, when we remember that the Master himself was brought up as a village carpenter and the majority of his disciples were workers with their hands.[11]

Whether or not T. W. Manson is correct in arguing for a different Aramaic word behind mathetes, we must agree that for Jesus leadership training was more a matter of apprenticeship than scholarship.

It is interesting to note that the emphasis on theoretical learning in the Rabbinic schools was actually foreign to Old Testament faith. As Rengstorf points out, "The theological attitude... is a Greek or Hellenistic attitude rather than a Jewish one, since in it the intellectual becomes the predominant principle and there is a falling short of the whole man".[12] Similar to our church educational institutions today, the Rabbis took over a Greek academic model and in doing so unknowingly assumed a foreign concept of personality and virtue.

Because of Jesus' different approach, he didn't establish a rival school in a large city as was the Rabbinic custom. Rather, he taught the disciples as they were "on the way" as Mark puts it (8:27; 9:33-34; 10:32). Jesus' method of training could not take place in the isolation of the classroom because it involved and intertwined many elements - demonstration, teaching, involvement in ministry, interaction, reflection, and prayer.

Jesus' training style also ran completely contrary to the elitist attitude of the Rabbinic school system.[13] To the chagrin of the Pharisees, he freely associated with the worst of sinners (Matt. 9:10) and even included a tax collector among his twelve disciples (Mark 2:14). In identifying with outsiders and common people, Jesus spoke in the vernacular Aramaic and used teaching devices which made learning easier for non-literate persons. Klem has an excellent extended discussion of this in his book *Oral Communication of the Scripture*. He compares Jesus to his contemporary Rabbis, saying:

> The Essenes and Pharisees, though perhaps sincere in their desire to teach the Law to all men, demanded that the people come to their institutions, learn their special language, memorize a large corpus of material, and learn the cantillation style of the teacher all as prerequisites for learning their 'important' teachings. They required that the people be extracted from their popular modes of expression and learn the skills of a special mode of communication before this new information could become available. The Pharisees also required a certain change in conduct prior to learning the message, as well as the willingness to acquire a new identification as non-Am-ha-ares. . . . In contrast to the communicative policies of the scholarly minority, Christ took upon himself the social identity of the majority. He used their popular system of oral communication. He accepted their level of knowledge as sufficient preparation for Him to explain to them the necessary information to produce spiritual maturity.[14]

In contrast to his contemporaries, Jesus did not require his disciples to learn archaic languages or scholarly terminology. He taught in the vernacular. He assumed that the profound truths of God's kingdom were best communicated using simple stories that his disciples could easily learn and use in their own ministry experiences.

In concluding this discussion we should note that Jesus didn't totally reject the Rabbinic teaching system. Even though he strongly condemned their elitist system (Matt. 23:8-12), their corpus of tradition (Mark 7:1-13), and their hyprocrisy (Matt. 23:23-32; Mark 8:15), still Jesus can praise the virtues of the scribe-become-disciple:

> Therefore every teacher of the law who has been instructed about the kingdom of heaven is like the owner of a house who brings out of his storeroom new treasures as well as old (Matt. 13:52).

This verse concludes a collection of parables related to the kingdom and so proclaims that the Rabbinic student who has become a follower of Christ can bring true treasures out of his previous learning. Jesus also affirms the potential value of scribal learning in Matt. 23, the very passage which is an extended condemnation directed at the teachers of the law. Near the end of the discourse Jesus declares,

> You snakes! You brood of vipers! How will you escape being condemned to hell? Therefore I am sending you prophets and wise men (sophous - scholars) and teachers (grammateis - scribes, instructors). Some of them you will kill and crucify; others you will flog in your synagogues and pursue from town to town (vv. 33,34).

In Jesus' phrase, "I am sending you. . . wise men and teachers," we can discover a dramatic affirmation of the role and calling of the Christian scholar. All of this shows us that Jesus was not condemning scholarly learning per se. In fact, perhaps we can hear him saying it has its important place. His overall example and teaching demonstrate, however, that he considered the scholarly, cognitive approach used in the Rabbinic schools to be an ineffective method for leadership training. That type of learning may have its place, and certain individuals could have a special calling to pursue it, but Jesus chose a radically different approach as the primary method of equipping leaders for ministry.

Jesus' example should challenge us today. Have we for too long tried to use a secular educational model for kingdom purposes? Does our emphasis on graduate training and scholarly degrees resemble the elitist Rabbinic system? Could it be that Jesus' methods are in fact the most effective? Do we have the courage, as Jesus had, to freely lay aside established and respected training patterns in order to use more dynamic methods of leadership training?

Jesus Offered Power for Witness and Ministry

Even with three years of intensive training from the Master Teacher, the disciples were ill-equipped for the tasks of ministry until their empowering by the Spirit on the day of Pentecost. In each of the commissions of the risen Christ, the presence and power of the Spirit are promised for the mission ahead (Matt. 28:18-20; Luke 24:45-49; John 20:21-22; and Acts 1:8). The importance of the Spirit for ministry is also emphasized in the extended discourse of Jesus in John 14-16.

Just as Christ had been anointed and empowered for ministry (Luke 3:21-22), so his followers would soon be energized by the Holy Spirit for the task ahead (Acts 1:8). Coleman says it graphically:

> We can understand why he charged the disciples to tarry until they be endued with power. How else could they ever do his work? The exalted Christ needed to become a living reality in their lives. The Enabler of his Kingdom mission had to fully possess them, purifying their hearts and directing their thoughts. Unless they were enthralled by his Presence, the work of their Lord would never thrill their souls. Nothing less than a personal baptism of fire, an enduement of power from on High, would suffice for the task at hand.[15]

Today we must realize that effective leadership training involves much more than informational learning, techniques, and interpersonal skills, important as these may be. Equipping for ministry requires empowering by the Spirit of God.

We must emphasize both initial and ongoing filling of the Spirit (Luke 11:13; Ephesians 5:18). Our training should nurture a dependence on the Spirit, an intimacy with this Counselor, a sensitivity to God's voice. Then Christ will indeed continue his work in and through us.

3. Paul's Success in Training Leaders

Paul's pattern of leadership training demands our attention not only because it is one of our prime biblical examples, but also because of its obvious success. Paul's ability to equip leaders enabled him to expand his ministry incredibly and leave behind him churches which would grow and multiply in the years and generations which followed.

Like Jesus, Paul was very much involved in choosing and equipping leaders. Throughout his missionary career Paul effectively trained two types of leaders: leaders of local churches and associates who traveled with and assisted him.

Paul's Overall Pattern

Paul's leadership training methods were remarkably like those Jesus used. There are the following crucial similarities:

1. Rejection of the Rabbinic pattern of education. As Jesus had done, Paul discarded this established technique in order to utilize methods clearly suited to his objectives. This deviation from the cultural norm is especially significant in Paul's example since he was rabbinically trained and could have easily chosen this residential and cognitive approach.

2. In-service training. Paul equipped leaders through observation and supervised involvement in actual ministry.

3. Prayer and fasting. Just as fasting had been a part of Jesus' and Paul's calling and preparation for ministry (Luke 4:1f; Acts 9:9ff, 13:2f), we find Paul fasting as he selects and commissions workers (Acts 14:23). Paul's letters also illustrate the rich prayer life he and his associates practiced (e.g., 1 Cor. 1:4; Eph. 1:15ff, 3:14ff; Phil. 1:3ff; Col. 1:3ff; 1 Thess. 1:2f; 2 Thess. 1:11ff).

4. The relational learning process. Training depended more on the depth and quality of relationships than on the amount of knowledge amassed - relationships with God, one another, and those served. Their intensive ministry sprang from a deep experience of God through prayer, was sustained by a close-knit team, and was in continued interaction with needy people.

The repeated surfacing of these four factors emphasizes their importance in leadership training. Rather than repeat them in this chapter, we will look at three of Paul's distinctive emphases: identification, modeling, and confidence in others.

Identification

Paul demonstrated an amazing ability to identify with others, to befriend them and win their love and esteem. This permeated his whole ministry including his training of leaders. His desire to identify with others sprang from his own experience of Christ.[16] Because Christ had identified himself with sinful man, Paul could say that Christ "loved me and gave himself for me" (Gal. 2:20). In response to this tremendous love Paul sought to identify himself fully with Christ (Phil. 3:7ff).

Just as Paul's view of Christ was transformed upon his conversion, so his view of all people was radically changed (2 Cor. 5:16). The love which moved Christ to identify with Paul now moved Paul to identify with all, in order to share this love (1 Cor. 9:19ff). Paul writes to the Thessalonians: "We loved you so much that we were delighted to share with you not only the gospel of God but our lives as well, because you had become so dear to us" (1 Thess. 2:8).

Paul's longing to identify with others out of his love for Christ infused his training efforts. He addresses Timothy, as well as Titus, as "my true son" (1 Tim. 1:2; Titus 1:4). Other terms Paul uses to describe associates disclose the depth of their relationships. Caird graphically expresses it:

> T.R. Glover has pointed out the significance of Paul's syn-compounds in this connection. Fourteen fellow workers are mentioned by name in his letters, four fellow prisoners, two fellow soldiers, two fellow slaves, one yokefellow. The Philippians have shared in his work as partners, and are invited to share in his imitation of Christ; and some women among them have shared his "athletic struggle". "The dearest of all ties for Paul is to find men sharing things with him. The work, the 'athletic life', the yoke, the slavery, the imitation - these are all expressions of his relation with Jesus Christ, the very essence of life; how much more it is to him when he finds his friends standing with him in that great loyalty!" (Glover, *Paul of Tarsus*, p. 180). And what it must have meant to his friends to share a prison cell with him, to fight the good fight of faith shoulder to shoulder with him, to bow the knee at his side as slaves of the one Lord! One example of Paul's gracious treatment of others is to be found in the salutations of his Epistles, where he always places beside his own name that of any friend known to the church who happens to be with him at the time of writing. In all his vast labours Paul never had any assistants or underlings - only partners and colleagues.[17]

Paul's principle of identification shows us that deep interaction and sharing in actual ministry is crucial in effective leadership training.

Modeling

Closely related to the principle of identification and frequently tied together in Paul's letters is the concept of modeling. Paul writes to the Galatians, "I plead with you, brothers, become like me, for I became like you" (Gal. 4:12). Paul held up his life as a model for his converts (2 Thess. 3:7ff), for local leaders (Acts 20:31), and for his younger partners (2 Tim. 3:10). It is obvious from the Epistles that lifestyle modeling was a very deliberate part of Paul's strategy. He encourages the Christians at Thessalonica to "imitate" (Greek *mimeomai*) the example he has set (2 Thess. 3:7,9). In the same way he exhorts the Corinthians to become his "imitators" (1 Cor. 4:16). Then he again tells them, "Become imitators of me, just as I am of Christ (own translation of 1 Cor. 11:1). In the same way, he asks those at Philippi to become "co-imitators" in following his example (Phil. 3:17). Paul realized that people need more than to be *taught* how to live, they need to be *shown.*

Just as Paul held out his life as a "model" (Greek *tupos*), so he expected his converts and assistants to become models to others. As the Christians at Thessalonica became imitators of Paul, his co-workers and the Lord, they themselves "became a model to all the believers in Macedonia and Achaia" (1 Thess. 1:6,7). Paul also commanded Timothy and Titus each to be a "model" to those they served (1 Tim. 4:12, Titus 2:4f).

We might envision Paul's concept of modeling like a stone dropped in a pond which sets in motion ever-widening wavelets. Christ's supreme example dropped into the reality of human history was transforming Paul's life whose example was impacting others and then extending to still others. This expansion of Christ's life in Paul's mind and practice involved modeling - living out the message and example of Christ.

This principle of modeling is repeated in leadership training throughout the New Testament: Jesus modeling attitudes and skills for his disciples (e.g., Mark 10:42ff); Barnabas serving as an example for Paul; Paul acting as a model for still other leaders.

Like identification, modeling far surpasses simple informational learning as a primary basis of training. It assumes the reality of close, caring relationships where ministry can be demonstrated and taught through actions and attitudes as well as information.

Confidence in Others

If we are to be as successful as Paul in reaching out to the world and training leaders, we must capture his attitudes - the heart and mind of Christ which motivated and shaped his mission. Paul's ability to identify with others flowed from the attitude of compassion - reaching out to people in response to Christ's love. His modeling was the result of affection, his desire to share the life of Christ which he himself experienced. Another key attitude of Paul was his confidence in Christ's continued work in others.

When the church at Corinth was plagued with strife and self-centeredness, Paul could still begin his letter by saying, "I always thank God for you because of his grace given you in Christ Jesus" (1 Cor. 1:4), following this with praise and affirmation of God's continued work in their lives (vv. 6-9). When the Galatian churches were going adrift, Paul could express confidence that they would return to the true understanding of the gospel (Gal. 5:10).

Paul's confidence in his associates impacted them. Caird expresses it like this:

> Men always admire those who bring out the best in them, and this Paul did for all with whom he associated because he always expected the best from them. He spared them as little as he spared himself, and they responded to his infectious enthusiasm.[18]

Paul realized that Christ's love encourages others and stands behind them. "It always protects, always trusts, always hopes, always perseveres" (1 Cor. 13:4). No doubt, Paul learned this truth in part from the acceptance and confidence extended to him by Barnabas (Acts 9:15f; 11:25f).

Roland Allen emphasizes our need to follow Paul's example by placing our confidence and faith in others:

> The power in which Paul was able to act in such boldness was the spirit of faith. Faith not in the natural capacities of his converts, but in the power of the Holy Ghost in them.
>
> Now if we are to practice any methods approaching to the Pauline methods in power and directness, it is absolutely necessary that we should first have this faith, this Spirit. Without faith - faith in the Holy Ghost, faith in the Holy Ghost in our converts -- we can do nothing. We cannot possibly act as the Apostle acted until we recover this faith. Without it we shall be unable to recognize the grace of the Holy Spirit in our converts, we shall never trust them, we shall never inspire in them confidence in the power of the Holy Spirit in themselves. If we have no faith in the power of the Holy Spirit in them, they will not learn to have faith in the power of the Holy Spirit in themselves. We cannot trust them, and they cannot be worthy of trust; and trust, the trust that begets trustworthiness, is the one essential for any success in the Pauline method.[19]

Leadership training requires more than proper methods and

perfected techniques. We also need a radical faith in the Holy Spirit which becomes a vibrant confidence in potential leaders.

Effective Leadership Training Today

In recent years a "new" concept is friendship evangelism. In our churches we have discovered that effective evangelism involves a lot more than dispensing information and asking for a response. It requires reaching out to others with concern and establishing and deepening friendships where Christ's good news and love can be shared. The key factor in caring and communicating is relationships.

The same principle is true in leadership training. For both Jesus and Paul, developing leaders meant bringing persons into meaningful, sharing relationships, involving them in actual ministry; modeling values, priorities, and skills; instilling vision and confidence; nurturing a dependence on God and responsiveness to his voice.

Today this calls us to a transformation in our concept of leadership training. Pastors and other leaders, persons full of faith and the Holy Spirit, should bring potential leaders into relationships where they can serve, learn, laugh, and grow side by side. Through ministry and sharing, fellowship with God can be modeled and priorities and skills demonstrated. This is the heart of successful training and growth.

4. Leadership Training in the Mennonite Church: Yesterday, Today, and the Future

Having seen the dynamic biblical principles for leadership training we now turn to the specific context of the Mennonite church. We will look at the most pressing issues: What concept of ministry shaped leadership roles and training in the early Anabaptist movement? What changes have occurred since then? What are the needs and principles that should guide our leadership training as we approach the 21st century?

The Early Anabaptists

When the Anabaptist movement blazed across central Europe in the 16th century it carried with it a revolutionary concept of ministry. Rejecting the "status clergy" concept of the state churches, the Anabaptists reclaimed the New Testament concept of the priesthood of all believers. They boldly declared that each Christian was a witness and minister of Christ. While affirming that the ministry belonged to the total church, the Anabaptists recognized from the earliest stages the need for definite congregational leadership, a person referred to in the 1527 Schleitheim Confession as "the Shepherd" (*der Hirt*). Article number 5 of the Confession states:

> The shepherd in the church shall be a person according to the rule of Paul, fully and completely, who has a good report of those who are outside the faith. The office of such a person shall be to read and exhort and teach, warn, admonish, or ban in the congregation, and properly to preside among the sisters and brothers in prayer, and in the breaking of the bread, and in all things to take care of the body of Christ, that it may be built up and developed, so that the name of God might be praised and honored through us, and the mouth of the mocker be stopped. He shall be supported, wherein he has need, by the congregation which has chosen him, so that he who serves the gospel can also live therefrom as the Lord has ordered.[20]

In the first twenty years of the Anabaptist movement the leadership roles were varied and flexible. Besides the position of shepherd other leaders are described with diverse titles such as "preacher, admonisher, minister, prophet, servant of the poor, treasurer, deacon, leader, overseer, teacher, and elder".[21] Function rather than position was considered crucial and a multiplicity of duties arose in response to individual giftedness and specific church need.

How were leaders trained in this initial period? Our information is limited. Apparently, there was no set pattern for training leaders. As gifts were recognized and utilized, preachers learned from practical experience, perhaps aided by older and more experienced leaders. Their writings evidence that they were persons of prayer who avidly studied the Scriptures.

Changes in Leadership

In the last half of the 16th century, Anabaptist leadership concepts experienced significant changes. The most profound change was that the church instead of continuing to spread began to withdraw. As persecution took its toll and the believers withdrew from urban involvement to rural seclusion, vision faded and faith was seen as a culture to be defended rather than good news to be shared. When the Anabaptist vision faded, the function of leaders shifted from visionary outreach to spiritual maintenance of the church.

As Jesus' and Paul's examples illustrate, vision is the most crucial factor in leadership training. It shapes and motivates and must be communicated to young leaders. Perhaps the main reason the

Anabaptist vision dimmed was the lack of effective leadership training.

Another significant change in the 16th century was the crystallization of leadership roles into the three offices of elder/bishop, preacher, and deacon, with any previous roles absorbed into these positions.[22] This subsequent pattern has been called "the three-fold plural lay ministry." Harder describes it:

> Congregations typically had one or several elders who were responsible for order, the "ministry of the Word," and the administration of the ordinances of baptism and the Lord's Supper. They had several preachers who assisted the elder in the administration of the ordinances, and then there were deacons who assisted the preacher in the reading of the Scriptures and the opening prayer.[23]

As roles became ossified, a plurality of leadership was retained but the Anabaptist vision of the priesthood of all believers faded. The leaders, rather than being equippers and motivators whose example and teaching guided the outreaching church, were now maintainers of the church.

A third change related to leaders was their educational level. Many of the first Anabaptist leaders were well educated. They had been trained as priests, university professors, or for some other profession. Many of these prime leaders were soon executed. In the years that followed, a negative view towards education developed. Perhaps this was because the academically trained authorities of the state church vehemently persecuted the Anabaptists and theologically explained away what the Anabaptists could see was the simple truth of the Bible. Also the state church clergy, though better educated, were often immoral and worldly. Smith notes the sixteenth century state church condition: "Among frequent charges brought against various clergymen were wife beating, frequenting taverns, gambling, excessive drinking, fighting, pride, and general neglect of duty."[24] Because of this the Anabaptists belittled formal educational credentials and stressed instead the necessity for mature and upright leaders.

The North American Experience

We now turn to the experience of Mennonites in North America. As Mennonites migrated to the United States and Canada from the seventeenth to the twentieth centuries, they brought with them the same three-fold concept of ministry that had prevailed in

Europe. In this system leadership and preaching responsibilities were plural rather than centered in one person. Leaders were called from the local church and were self-supporting. Very few received any training.

In the past century, especially recent decades, this has changed. As time passed and the educational level of the general populace increased, the need for biblical and theological training presented itself more and more to Mennonite churches and their leaders. At first they sought this training by attending the denominational schools of other groups or interdenominational Bible institutes. Eventually, though, different Mennonite colleges and seminaries were established.

As the educational level of leaders has changed so has their overall role. The plural form of ministry has been almost entirely replaced by the single-pastor model. Instead of having several persons (bishops and preachers) in each church sharing preaching and pastoral oversight, these functions now belong to one person. There are still deacons (or elders), but instead of being appointed for life they are elected for terms of several years.

Whatever we make of the shift from the plural ministry to the one-person pastoral model, it is clear that the change has taken place without adequate reflection. Leland Harder says,

> Evidence of the unthinking way the mono-pastoral pattern has been adopted in the General Conference Mennonite Church without adequate respect for our history is the way our training institutions were structured from the start to staff constituent congregations with professional pastors following a mainstream Protestant model without a serious critique of how they are to function within a historic believers' church tradition.[25]

Harder's study shows that in the shift to the one-pastor system we unknowingly took over deficient concepts of ministry and leadership foreign to our heritage and the New Testament. At the same time he points out that there is a new realization that ministry is the task of the whole church. At the same time, there is a new appreciation of the important role of pastoral leaders "to equip God's people for work in his service, to the building up of the body of Christ" (Eph. 4:12, NEB).

Harder's observations concur with my own and others'. From a biblical and Anabaptist perspective there is a new vision for ministry as belonging to the whole people of God and there is a call for strong, plural forms of leadership. The inadequate and narrowly defined concept of "the ministry" has begun to give way to the rich

New Testament understanding in this area. Another assumption, however, remains unchallenged. That is the unstated, but primary, assumption that academic learning is the normative method for training church leadership. In other words we have asked, "What is the New Testament concept of ministry?" and begun to realize its radical implications. But perhaps an equally important question is being overlooked: What are the New Testament principles and methods for actually training leaders? In the final portion of this chapter I call our attention to the critical New Testament principles for evaluating and improving our leadership training as we look to the future.

New Testament Principles for Future Training

In chapter one we saw that Jesus spoke of sending scribes and scholars to proclaim his purposes (Matt. 23:34). This demonstrates that Jesus did not condemn scholarly learning but recognized its potential value (Matt. 13:52). At the same time, we know that both Jesus and Paul rejected the residential, formal school system that other teachers of their time used.

Putting together Jesus' affirmation of scholarly learning and his rejection of a structured residential schooling, we can conclude two things: 1) that academic learning is important and should be encouraged; and 2) that it should not be our sole or even primary form of leadership training. The fact that we have come to rely almost solely on this model forces us to look at the key issues. Three key New Testament principles that must guide us in the present and the future relate to: 1) the trainers; 2) the setting; and 3) the goal of training.

The Trainers

In the New Testament church leaders trained leaders. Jesus modeled ministry for the disciples. Barnabas equipped Paul. Paul instructed Timothy and other young leaders. As this took place the learners assimilated the skills and lifestyles of their teachers. The disciples continued the preaching and healing ministry of Jesus. Paul and his associates carried forward the cross-cultural church planting thrust that had been learned from Barnabas. When our goal is to develop mature, effective pastors for local churches, our learners must work in vital ministry relationships with successful, competent pastors. Whatever leaders we are developing -- evangelists, teachers, church planters -- the way that they most effectively learn the necessary skills is through involvement with effective leaders in ministry. On the other hand, if the primary model we set before students is academic professors, they will tend to assimilate this style of ministry.

The need is not so much for programs to place learners in mentor relationships as it is for leaders in ministry to follow the example of Jesus and Paul and give their *best* efforts -- their time, attention and prayer -- to equipping others. This means bringing them into relationships of friendship and ministry where values, skills, and attitudes are caught not just taught.

Those of us who are in ministry must be very deliberate in following Jesus' example of choosing potential leaders - working with them, praying for them, placing confidence in them, and involving them in ministry. Jesus continually ate, traveled and ministered with others. In doing so he was involved in an ongoing process of training leaders through interacting, modeling, teaching, encouraging and correcting. He serves as our example for effective equipping ministry.

The Setting

In the New Testament examples persons learned in the context of actual ministry rather than in a classroom setting. The most important feature of this is that learners gained the precise skills that would be needed in their own ministries later. Formal classroom education teaches a certain set of skills. Although there is some overlap, these are not the same skills needed for pastoral and other leadership ministries. I believe that this was the main reason that Jesus and Paul rejected the Rabbinic model.

Here we must realize that the method is the message. Students will attempt to master the skills required in our training methods, assuming that these are the same skills that will later be important in ministry. The academic set-up teaches a person to study, think and write clearly -- important ministry skills. At the same time, other crucial skills are not learned. Someone can graduate with flying colors while failing miserably in terms of maturity, prayer life, and relational skills. An excellent student can turn out to be a terrible pastor and the reverse is also possible.

When the context of training is removed from the ministry setting, as the classroom setting typically is, the process can in some ways actually short-circuit effectiveness in ministry. In my own experience after completing college and a graduate degree I had to unlearn an intellectual accent in order to preach more effectively in my congregation. Christian communicator Tim Timmons relates the same experience in his own striving to speak to people's needs. In his article "Why Should They Listen to Me?", he says,

A box is formed by our influential professors and past

mentors. The first few years out of seminary I found myself still speaking, writing, and counseling for my professors. It was as if they were still with me, looking over my shoulder and evaluating me. This blurred my primary audience.[26]

Following the New Testament models will mean that the primary training setting will be real ministry. Training leaders in the context of in-depth ministry helps ensure that the right skills are being learned and that the content of teaching is being applied.

The Goal

In the New Testament examples the goal of leadership training was relational rather than informational. The core of the academic model is to teach persons *to know*. The emphasis is on the cognitive - conveying information and teaching students to think. In taking over this system we have unconsciously assumed the same goals. By doing so we have embraced concepts of what knowledge and virtue are and who humans are that in many ways are foreign to the biblical concepts. Famous Brazilian educator Paulo Freire has pointed to the deficiency of these Hellenistic educational assumptions. He says, "Socratic intellectualism mistook the definition of the concept for knowledge of the thing, and this knowledge for virtue".[27]

Our schools, like the Rabbinic ones, emphasize teacher- student, student-student relationships. But even with these relationships, the school setting is a context where cognitive learning, rather than relationships, is at the center. The educational experience can in fact be alienating rather than relationship building. Augustine, who could be considered the dean of the first real seminary, was the first to point this out. He emphasized Paul's words, "Knowledge puffs up, but love builds up".[28]

Arthur Henderson has also pointed out the potential harm of education divorced from the relational context:

> There is a great danger in giving training in various useful functions and techniques and calling it leadership training without dealing adequately with human relationships, including insights into the trainee's own feelings and behaviour. In groups outside the church it is frequently found that the very knowledge of, and competence in, functional tasks blinds would-be leaders to their failures in human relations, either because they fail to diagnose the situation, especially feelings toward the task, the organization, or the claimant to authority, or because they fail to maintain the goodwill and confidence of others in their leadership.[29]

The primary goal of Jesus and Paul was to teach potential leaders to relate. Because their training approach was centered in prayer and immersed in ministry it demanded growth in relationships, not merely with the instructor and other learners but also with God and those being served. There were many elements in their training methods - modeling, supervised ministry involvements, cognitive learning, correction and encouragement - but in all this the ultimate goal was that they relate to God, experiencing his grace and power, and then relate to the world in compassionate outreach. Jesus taught potential leaders that without quality relationships ministry would be fruitless (John 15:5-17). Paul says similarly that if we don't learn to love, all our knowledge amounts to nothing (1 Cor. 13:2).

If we take the New Testament teaching and examples seriously, our ultimate training goal will be to train leaders to relate to God and others; this goal will have profound implications for the trainers, setting and methods we choose for effective leadership training.

5. Field Research on the Call to Pastoral Ministry

Scope of Research

This chapter reports the findings of my own field research into the call to pastoral ministry. For my master's thesis I wanted to discover which factors were most significant in the calling process. I interviewed six pastors in depth, then sent out questionnaires to all fifty-six Illinois Mennonite pastors of English-speaking churches, both Illinois Conference (MC), and Central District Conference (GC). Forty-two (or seventy-five percent) returned a completed questionnaire. I include in this briefer study only the questions and responses that were most significant.

Survey Results   <u>Average</u>

2. What age were you when you first felt called or decided to enter pastoral ministry?   23.2

5. How did the following persons or factors influence your initial call or decision to enter pastoral ministry? (Listed below are the total points received from responses indicated on a scale of -3 to +3.)

Involvement in practical ministry experience _____ 80

Pastor _____ 63

Other persons in local church_____ 57

Personal crisis or religious experience_____ 55

Family_____ 51

College or seminary teachers _____ 48

S.S. teachers_____ 31

Local training program _____ 20

Youth Leader _____ _____ 17

16. Has the discernment and development of pastoral leaders from within the congregation(s) where you have served been a high priority and a deliberate part of your ministry?

	Percentages
Yes, definitely	61.0
Only somewhat	19.5
No, not significantly	19.5

17. In what specific ways have you encouraged persons to consider pastoral ministry or develop skills in this area? (Listed total who mentioned these items.)

Provided practical experience _____11

Encouragement to consider/pursue pastoral ministry __10

Encouraged persons to get academic training _____ 9

Leadership training _____ 8

Personal counsel _____ 7

Gift discernment _____ 4

Financial support for schooling _____ 2

Encourage persons to take local training courses _____ 2

Take seminary students in
    supervised ministry program _____ 2

Pray for them _____ 1

18. How many persons that you know of have entered pastoral
    ministry significantly influenced by you in this decision?
    (Categorised according to the response to question 16,
    "Has the development of pastoral leaders been a high-
    priority in your ministry?")

	Total number influenced to ministry	Average per pastor
25 respondents answering "yes"	61	2.4
8 respondents answering "only somewhat"	4	.5
8 respondents answering "no"	6	.75

Results of Research

The responses to the questionnaire indicate that a person's call
to pastoral ministry typically occurs at a very young age, the average
being 23.2. Question five in the survey yielded the most important
findings. The three most important factors in discerning a call to
ministry were practical ministry experience (80 points), the pastor
(63), and other church members (57). This surprised me. The fact
that these three ranked higher than such key elements as religious
experience (55) and family (51) shows the importance of actual
involvement in ministry and the crucial role of the pastor and congregation in the discernment and calling process.

Findings from the final section revealed that a majority of pastors consider the development of pastoral leaders a high priority in their ministries and that those who do have considerably more impact in this area as a result. A variety of different methods were mentioned as ways to help develop pastoral leaders. A close look reveals, however, that while several pastors and congregations work very intentionally at developing leaders, overall there is a lack of deliberate training and discipling on a local church level. One encouraging development that several churches which were surveyed reported is a rediscovery of the plurality of leadership ministry. In these congregations deacons (or elders) and others are being trained and used to serve in areas such as visitation, preaching and counseling which previously were the sole responsibility of the pastor.

Implications for Leadership Training Today

Because practical ministry was by far the most significant factor in these pastors' calls, we must take even more seriously the New Testament training principle of learning in the midst of ministry. This is where gifts are discovered, skills developed, and weaknesses revealed. Persons who are possibly called to ministry should not be sent off to school in the hope that they will discern their call there. Although this may sometimes happen, the ideal setting for discerning and affirming this call is in the context of actual ministry with the help and support of the pastor and local congregation. Direction for other training can then arise from this process of discerning gifts and ministries.

The field research also pointed to the vital role of the pastor in influencing persons toward pastoral ministry. My findings here correspond to other studies which have consistently indicated the pastor as the most important person influencing individuals' decisions to pursue ministry.[30] Pastors must follow the example of Christ and take the initiative in pastoral and other leadership training seeing this as perhaps the most important area of their ministry, that with the greatest impact and longest lasting results. The survey particularly indicates the need to work with young persons developing relationships with them, involving them in ministry opportunities, praying for them, and encouraging them to consider prayerfully pastoral and other ministry possibilities at an early age.

This survey has revealed that many positive things are happening in our churches in calling and preparing leaders. At the same time it shows the need for clearer understanding and more deliberate efforts in leadership training.

6. Modern Trends in Ministerial Training

Around the world ministerial training is experiencing tremendous changes. This is especially true in third world countries where growing churches accelerate the need for capable leaders. In the vast diversity of situations creative and effective approaches have emerged and established programs have been changing. In North America, too, there have been rumblings and beginnings of change.

The purpose of this chapter is to look at the current rethinking of ministerial training. We want to understand and evaluate these current trends so that we can apply relevant insights in our own task of calling and equipping leaders.

Theological Education by Extension

Theological Education by Extension (TEE) is by far the most important and far-reaching recent development in third world ministerial training. Although it is only now beginning to impact North America, TEE was first used in 1963 by Presbyterians in Guatemala. Since that time the movement has spread around the world. At the beginning of this decade it included from 300 to 400 programs with perhaps 100,000 students.[31] No doubt, the numbers would now be even greater.

What is TEE? Extension education stands in contrast to residential schooling. Whereas residential schools, such as seminaries or Bible colleges, have students come to them in order to study, extension programs take learning to the location of the students. This is done by giving the students materials such as textbooks, assignments, cassettes, etc. which they study on their own. Typically, they gather weekly for a class/seminar with other students and an instructor to discuss and integrate their learnings. Since the class, instructor, and studies are extended to the students' location, rather than vice versa, students can continue in their natural relationships, work situations, and church responsibilities.

What "Extension" Means

The "extension" in Theological Education by Extension has been understood geographically, that is, the geographic extension of studies to further locations. Educators involved in TEE, however, call us to a broader understanding of "extension" because TEE "extends" in other crucial ways.[32] In order to be as effective as possible the attempt is made to extend theological education in each of the following ways:

1. Geographically. Teaching and training is decentralized to

make learning available in as many locations as possible.

2. Chronologically. Classes are scheduled at the most convenient times for the students. Persons with typical jobs might prefer very early morning or evening classes. Pastors or other church workers are busy on weekends and find weekdays best. Schedules are more flexible in farm communities but they should avoid planting and harvest seasons.

3. Culturally. The residential school has a diversity of cultural backgrounds in each class. The extension class reaches the culture of one locale and in content and approach can address its specific concerns.

4. Academically. Ideally, extension programs offer courses at all academic levels represented in the churches they serve. Kinsler diagrams the extension model in its third world context like this:[33]

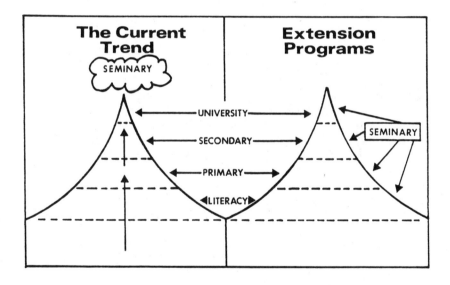

As this illustrates, traditional ministerial training has been seen as the final stage in a long educational process. This has greatly restricted the number of trained leaders. It has also often created an elitist tendency distancing pastors from those they serve. In contrast, extension education offers classes and materials to people at as many academic levels as possible. Students at all levels are given equal recognition for ministry.

5. Economically. Extension education can reach persons from

a much wider range of social and economic backgrounds because it does not remove them from productive jobs only to place on them the further expense of room and board at a residential school. This is especially important for persons with families to support.

6. Ecclesiastically. In extension education learning becomes more church-centered rather than largely abstract. Learning also is made available to a much wider variety of people rather than simply clergy. The concept of ministry is broadened to include the total people of God.

7. Numerically. TEE has readily trained more persons involved in the churches' leadership. Kinsler points out that extension programs reach:

> older as well as young people, women as well as men, non-clergy as well as candidates for the ministry and church workers, people from all academic levels, sub-cultures, and social-economic groups. This is not merely a quantitative concern but ideological and theological also. The ministry should involve the whole body of Christ and serve all sectors of human society. Theological education by extension facilitates the formation of ministry of the people, by the people, and for the people.[34]

TEE extends training to church leaders geographically, chronologically, culturally, academically, economically, ecclesiastically, and numerically to root it more deeply in congregational life and ministry. The result is an educational approach radically different from the traditional residential school. Kinsler [35]illustrates the contrast like this:

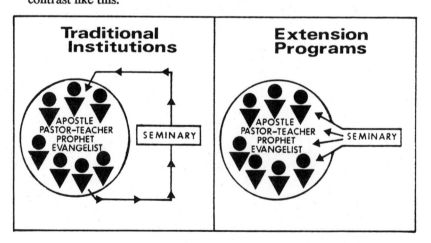

As this illustrates, traditional ministerial training has required persons to leave their natural setting and church relationships in order to enroll in a residential school. After years of costly academic training the persons are then artificially plugged back into the church with a new role and status. Extension programs, on the other hand, move training into the life of the church to equip the leadership and people of God already there for ministry. In the process the number and diversity of students is expanded and learning can be immediately integrated into congregational ministry and outreach.

By extending education to more people, further locations, new academic levels, and placing it firmly in church life, TEE has not only expanded training possibilities but also has contributed to new concepts of ministry. TEE challenges traditional methods on both practical and theological grounds.

Advantages of Theological Education by Extension

In the initial stages of the TEE movement the advantages put forward had largely to do with quantity. Many more persons could be trained than with residential schools. Extension education cost far less. Churches grew faster in areas where TEE was used. Now extension education is being promoted on the basis of quality as well for theological and educational reasons.

Theologically, TEE is commended because it goes much farther in training the *right* people, because it teaches persons who are called by their local church and are already in ministry. Residential schools, on the other hand, have generally accepted anyone academically qualified. Often these have been young people whose call was not discerned by the church and who may not have been gifted for leadership ministry. Ted Ward and Sam Rowen have stated, "Extension programs are much more in the business of serving those men who *are* called by the church rather than those who claim to be called or those who hope to be called once they 'make the grade'".[36]

Kinsler says it like this:

> The Western churches, whatever their concept of the ministry may be, have developed an academic-professional model of ministry which is self-defeating in terms of effective leadership. Within this system theological education serves to select young, inexperienced men and women, separate them from the normal processes of leadership formation, and place them artificially over the other members.
>
> Theological education by extension recognizes that leaders

are best formed and selected among their peers in the on-going life of the church and society and offers to these emerging leaders the resources of ministerial training within that context[37].

Educationally TEE offers several qualitative benefits. This is because learners are not removed from ministry relationships and responsibilities. The advantages of this are supported by modern educational theory which teaches that a high quality curriculum for the training of professionals contains three parts: cognitive input, field experiences, and interactive seminars. The connection between these three parts can be illustrated by drawing a two rail fence.[38]

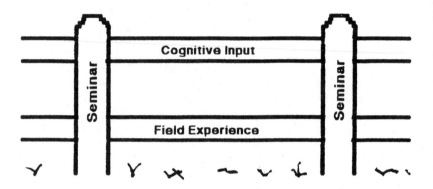

As illustrated by this model, it is important that the cognitive input and field experience occur simultaneously for then application, retention, and motivation are greatly increased. When the student can make direct application of new knowledge to experience, it is more useful and more likely to be remembered. Motivation is also increased because the student sees the immediate value of the studies. So both aspects of this educational process, the cognitive and experiential, are greatly enriched when occurring side by side.

As the fence model illustrates, the seminar serves to make a solid connection between cognitive input and field experiences. There instructors and students can share and discuss how new knowledge relates to the work in which they are involved. They can work together at problem solving and evaluation. Educators have said, "The hallmarks of a good seminar are the occasions and stimulations to reflect upon and evaluate learnings from both cognitive input and from the field experiences, with a premium on relating the two".[39]

Jesus' and Paul's training methods correspond to the rail fence model. They gave their learners cognitive instruction as well as actual experience in ministry. As in the model, these two aspects were united through interaction and supervision. Both on theological and educational grounds, TEE challenges us in North America to integrate informational learning and ministry experience into real congregational life and outreach.

The North American Scene

The primary approach to ministerial training in the U.S. and Canada is residential schooling. In most denominations the normal level of this training is postgraduate education. This has not always been the case. In fact, residential theological education is a very recent phenomenon. Throughout history the vast majority of pastors and priests in all church traditions were trained on the job. Robert Michaelsen reports the situation earlier in this century:

> An analysis of the 1926 Religious Census figures for seventeen of the largest white Protestant denominations in the United States showed that over 40 percent of the ministers of these denominations were graduates of neither college nor of theological seminary, while only 33% were graduates of both. Actually these figures are high since the census bureau was very liberal in its interpretation of the meaning of college or seminary.[40]

The change from supervised, experiential training of ministers to a schooling approach in major denominations has not taken place without some questions. Writing in 1848, Gardiner Spring urged that the best features of the previous system be retained. John Frame refers to Spring's out-of-print book:

> In 1848, after 34 years on the board of Princeton Theological Seminary, the Rev. Gardiner Spring wrote a book called *The Power of the Pulpit*, wherein he compared the generation of seminary-trained ministers with the older generation of pastorally-trained ministers. Though Spring had no interest in turning back the clock (realizing the practical impossibility of dissolving the seminaries and returning to the old system) and, indeed, deeply committed as he was to the work of Princeton, he reluctantly concluded that the older generation was notably superior to the younger in pastoral effectiveness and spiritual maturity. He advocated (1) that the seminary faculty maintain close supervision, not only over a student's academic

progress, but also over his social and spiritual development; (2) that the seminary faculty itself consist of men with extensive pastoral experience; (3) that no student be ordained to the ministry until he has spent a time of apprenticeship with an experienced pastor.[41]

More recently, the residential seminary approach has been challenged by numerous voices. H. R. Niebuhr has pointed out how easily the intellectual activity of the theological school can become dichotomized from the life of the student and the concerns of the church.[42] He calls for a deeper involvement of students in congregational life.

Professor Paul Holmer of Yale asked a question with the title of his article, "Can We Educate Ministers Scientifically?"[43] He points out the inherent tension between academic learning which requires neutrality and faith which demands commitment and passion. To bridge this gap Holmer suggests an internship of at least two years for the ministerial student. He says:

> Is it not time to consider anew a more active training of ministers in actual parish life? It seems to me that most ministerial candidates need both academic exposure and an active internship program under the most scrupulous direction. They need an opportunity to put their understanding of the gospel to immediate use. Furthermore, they need on-the-spot correction.[44]

Holmer also questions the necessity of seven years of study for all candidates, stating:

> We must explore the feasibility of shortening the course of ministerial study. There seems to be no good reason to require seven years of advanced work for the ministerial student. Certainly a four-year course leading to the Bachelor of Divinity degree would be sufficient. Ministerial training is not a deeper and deeper penetration into the field, and we have lost rather than gained by analogizing the training with that of other professions.[45]

Ray Stedman has gone farther by challenging the context of seminary education. He says:

> My real problem with seminaries is *how* they teach what they are teaching. ...they remove both students and faculty from

the normal stream of life and then wonder why both seem to grow dry and cold through the seminary experience. The Lord's method (and the apostles') was to take young men with them into all the various experiences of normal life and teach them in the midst of these experiences and by using the experiences as learning opportunities. Why do seminaries struggle endlessly to be like secular graduate schools with all the trappings of academia, when the apostolic method is far more efficient and effective? Put seminary training back where it belongs: into the churches, where skilled and able teachers and pastors would teach small, carefully selected bands of students in situations where both teachers and students would be deeply involved in life.[46]

The repeated criticism and plea is that ministerial training must be integrated into actual ministry experience and congregational life. Of course, the seminaries themselves have been recognizing this need and making positive changes. Practical in-service experiences are being more strongly encouraged, or required, through channels such as Clinical Pastoral Education, field education, or internships. Some seminaries have also begun using TEE to extend their programs.

Mennonite institutions and conferences are showing new creativity in the area of leadership training. A recent development in several areas has been Conference Based Theological Education. This moves seminary teachers to various locations to teach courses at a similar level to that offered on the campuses. Another new program at Hesston College, Hesston, Kansas, leads to a two-year Associate of Arts degree in Pastoral Ministries. This offers an attractive alternative for those called to pastoral leadership who cannot afford the time and financial commitment of a longer program. A strength of this program is its deliberate aim of training those persons whose call has emerged from ministry or involvement in congregational life. As their promotional brochure "A.A. in Pastoral Ministries", states:

The A. A. for Pastoral Ministries is for persons without a college degree who are either already in leadership within a congregation or who have been encouraged by the congregation to acquire training for pastoral ministry. Typically, such persons have maturity and experience within the church. The 'target person' for this program would be over 25 years old and would have received some sense of affirmation by the congregation.

Another positive development in several regional conferences is teacher-disciple programs. These programs give congregational leaders and members ministry skills by uniting the three elements which we saw earlier in the two-rail fence model:

1. Cognitive input, provided here through reading assignments and occasional workshops or classes.

2. Involvement in ministry, a specific ministry assignment which is tied to the program where the student's skills can be developed and evaluated.

3. Seminars, where interaction takes place on two levels in these programs to integrate the learning and development of the student. Regular supervision and support are offered by a teacher/mentor and periodic group meetings of all those involved in the program are held.

Assessment of Recent Trends in Ministerial Training

Modern trends in pastoral training are exciting and promising. They confirm what we have seen repeatedly in this study, that the equipping of pastoral leaders happens best when it is integrated into actual ministry experience and congregational life.

The movement in our seminaries to unite academic learning and ministry involvement through Clinical Pastoral Education, field experience and internships is to be praised and encouraged. At the same time, it should be noted a) that these additions are essentially appendages tied to a program which at its very core is academic and cognitive, and b) that the typical residential character of the school normally separates rather than unites the pastoral training and congregational ministry.

As Ross Kinsler has said:

> Schools can contribute to the intellectual and personal growth of their pupils, but leadership development takes place in society, in the group, in the life of the church. In recent years schools and seminaries have tried to provide more of an environment for integral development, with simulations and field experiences, but these are by and large sporadic and pale imitations of real life. And the socialization process of these institutions can be completely irrelevant or discontinuous or even negative as regards leadership in the churches.[47]

Recent attempts in our schools to bring together ministerial training and ministry experience may seem novel, or even radical. Yet the uniting of the two elements will require far more drastic changes. We have torn asunder what was once joined together. These elements must be brought together and married. Schools are in the process of bringing them closer. Right now, however, they are far from being married or even going steady. They are just beginning to date.

The new diversity of approaches to pastoral training is to be affirmed. We should not try to limit or over-standardize our methods.[48] Instead, we must diversify our methods to train leaders effectively at different levels, locations, contexts, and cultures to fully extend leadership training to all concerned.

7. A Strategy for Leadership Training

A Suit That Fits

Sometimes our leadership training efforts remind me of the man who wanted a new suit. He heard that there was an exceptional tailor in his town named Hans. He went to Hans, secured his services, and selected the best materials. One morning he picked up his new suit on the way to work. That same afternoon before going home he tried on the suit. Twisting and bending his body, he fit into the suit with great difficulty. The suit pulled him entirely out of shape; his back was hunched, one shoulder drooped, a leg was twisted. Unable to get out of his suit, the man started to go home. He hobbled out of the office and stumbled onto the bus. As he rode home, a bystander on the bus approached him and said, "Oh! Your suit must have been made by Hans the Tailor. Only Hans could make a suit for someone whose body is as deformed as yours!"

Just as the man's suit looked ideal to the bystander, so our training systems sometimes look like a perfect fit. What other methods could produce the graduates our institutions are now turning out, with such academic expertise and cyclopedic knowledge? Yet other questions are also crucial: Are we equipping pastors who are persons of prayer? Is their ability to think critically matched with a passion for the gospel? Can they relate to others sensitively and preach prophetically? How well do our training methods really "fit" our message and the needs of our churches and world?

This study has researched leadership training from many angles so that like a tailor taking measurements we might achieve a proper fit, leaders suited to the church of the future.

Taking Measurements for Leadership Training

We began by looking at the call and training of leaders from a New Testament perspective. Jesus and Paul gave leadership the highest priority. They rejected the residential, scholarly approach of the rabbinic schools. Their training meant leaders training leaders in the context of intensive ministry with an emphasis on prayer.

Next we looked at pastoral training in the experience of the Mennonite churches. The Anabaptists emphasized the importance of pastoral leadership. Although many of the very first Anabaptist leaders were educated, following generations relied for centuries on leaders with only minimal education or training. In the past century we have relied increasingly on academic schools to train our pastors. While this has brought improvements, biblical and practical considerations challenge us to integrate our training into congregational life and outreach. Field research on the experience of Illinois Mennonite pastors underscored the importance of practical ministry experience and the vital role of the local pastor and church in the calling of persons to pastoral ministry.

Finally, we saw that around the globe, especially in third world nations, ministry training is being revolutionized. Everywhere new efforts are being made to place training within the life of the local church. For both theological and educational reasons the key elements for equipping leaders - modeling, spiritual formation, practical experience, cognitive learning, and personal interaction - must be integrated into ministry relationships.

What has this study revealed? Repeatedly we have seen that dynamic leadership training means effective leaders training developing leaders in the context of actual ministry. When modeling, instructing and mentoring happen in this context, lives are shaped, callings clarified, gifts discerned, skills refined, and prayer deepened.

Leadership Training Suited to the Church of the Future

Our Mennonite conferences have been setting bold, new plans for outreach. We are responding afresh to God's call to make disciples of Christ and plant new churches. As we move ahead where will leaders come from for both new and existing congregations? The crucial ingredient is leadership training. The need is not for opportunities to work and share the Good News of Christ but for persons to take the lead in actually doing the work. As Jesus said, "The harvest is plentiful but the workers are few. Ask the Lord of the harvest, therefore, to send out workers into his harvest field" (Matt. 10:37-38). How do we work together to make the vision of dynamic leadership training a reality?

The Local Pastor

Pastors, along with church planters, missionaries, and other leaders, are the vital link in leadership training. As the New Testament reveals, the most effective setting for training is actual ministry, not the classroom and the most effective trainers are the church leaders, not academic instructors. Although most pastors consider the training of future leaders as important, almost none have worked deliberately and intensively at training leaders in the way that Jesus and Paul did. This is because we were not trained that way ourselves. Lacking this model we turn to the model we do know (the academic one) and encourage potential leaders to go off to school. We must relearn the biblical methods and recognize that we do have a model, Jesus himself. By following his example we can learn the skills of leadership training.

Pastors and other leaders, following Jesus' example, should work at leadership training at more than one level. As Jesus worked with the Twelve, the pastor should seek to train and involve a manageable number of persons in shepherding roles. Out of this group several should receive more intensive attention and instruction such as Jesus gave his three closest disciples.

As Jesus did, pastors must take the initiative. The pastor must pray intensely for the selection of these leaders (Luke 6:12) and for their continued growth. The primary focus of Jesus' prayers (and his life) was the calling and equipping of leaders (Matt. 9:37-38; Luke 22:32; John 17:9-19). As his death approached, Jesus interceded for his disciples: "I pray for them. I am not praying for the world, but for those you have given me for they are yours" (John 17:6). As he continued he prayed for their protection from the evil one, their joy, their purity, and their mission.

The goal of the training process must be clearly relational. It must not be seen primarily as a cognitive process where we are simply imparting knowledge and teaching persons how to think. The goal is relational. We want persons to deepen their walk with God and learn how to relate to others in caring ministry in the attitudes and power of Christ. If our goal is only cognitive we will simply gather persons in a classroom setting. If it is relational we will establish deep relationships of friendship, support and ministry.

Jesus' method of training leaders was to share life with them. They were with him as he ministered, ate, prayed and traveled. As he modeled ministry for them, they saw how he related to those in need and how he dealt with pressure and opposition. These disciples heard his teaching repeatedly and received their own instruction. As Jesus involved them in ministry they could come to him with questions and receive his correction and encouragement. Not only was Christ a support to them in their first ministry experiences, they were also a support to him and to one another. The pastor following Jesus' example will bring potential leaders alongside in all the variety of life and ministry activities - offering friendship, modeling, teaching, involvement in practical ministry, correction and encouragement.

It is obvious that this type of training will require an incredible amount of time and energy. Many will object, saying, "I'm too busy." Jesus and Paul were also busy. Their ministries were large and constantly growing. Yet it is staggering how much time they gave to leadership training. They were deeply involved in training others because they knew that it was the only way for their leaders to achieve lasting, far-reaching results.

Pastors also fail to do leadership training because they don't see potential leaders in the congregation. This is a "visual" problem. The leaders are there but the pastors don't see them. Remember that the twelve men that Jesus selected were not outstanding individuals. In the Gospels we are struck by their unbelief, self-centeredness, and inability to learn. They were chosen more for their potential than for their gifts or maturity. Jesus faced countless frustrations and painful disappointments in working with them, yet his efforts paid off. Jesus had faith in God and confidence in his disciples. Capturing that faith and confidence is essential for training future leaders.

Pastors and other leaders must move forward in discovering and developing potential leaders. They must engage them in ministry and instruction. They must model lives of prayer, service, and spiritual authority.

The Local Congregation

The examples of the New Testament church, the early Anabaptists, together with my own field research, highlight the importance of the local church in calling persons to leadership ministries. This process includes prayer and fasting, gift discernment, practical ministry experience and verbal encouragement.

There are two specific things that each congregation can do to make leadership training a reality. First, free the pastor to give more time to training leaders. This is important since in today's church the congregation often thinks of itself as the employer and the pastor as the employee. If there is a job description, leadership training should be very near the top. If almost half of Jesus' ministry as recorded in Mark was given to training, we must also give it a high priority. Secondly, a congregation should involve potential leaders in ministry responsibilities and offer financial support where appropriate.

Conferences

The regional conferences can advance leadership training by establishing and encouraging teacher-disciple programs which unite ministry, spiritual formation, instruction, and supervision in the context of church life and outreach. The programs like these that have been established have proven very effective. Some have floundered or been discontinued, however, for financial reasons. We must recognize that although these programs are expensive, they are far less costly than the established residential programs.

Another responsibility of the conferences should be to offer training to pastors on how to train others. Many pastors desire to train congregational leaders and potential pastors but don't know how to proceed. Also conferences should require discipling relationships between capable, experienced pastors and those just beginning pastoral ministry. The young pastor, possibly just out of college or seminary, is often essentially alone. Supervision and encouragement from a veteran pastor can offer perspective and wisdom. It can also prevent painful mistakes. Jesus sent the disciples out to minister two by two; ours go out unaccompanied.

Academic Institutions

At the beginning of this century Roland Allen, an Anglican missionary to China, challenged the established mission strategies. He called the churches to abandon their Western institutional approach to cross-cultural witness in order to follow simpler New Testament methods. No one listened. Allen was told that the biblical methods were impractical and outdated. Now, more than half a century later, many minds have been changed. Allen was right. Missions had naively assumed the methods and mindset of Western society. To the extent that mission strategy deviated from the New Testament principles, to that extent it became ineffective and oppressive.

I relate this story because in leadership training we have ignored the New Testament principles for too long. Our training programs have basically been a duplication of surrounding secular models.

Academic training is good and should be encouraged. It has benefited our churches significantly. However, we have expected it to carry too much of the responsibility of equipping leaders. If we are to unite real ministry and academic learning a new mindset and new methods are called for. In light of the New Testament principles, the history and needs of our churches, and the current rethinking of ministry training, I offer the following suggestions to our academic institutions seeking to train ministry leaders.

Develop a New Mindset

Rather than conforming to the patterns of this world we should seek transformation through a new mentality (Romans 12:2). We must give very careful attention to our underlying philosophies and goals. If our ultimate intention is equipping persons for ministry our goals will be relational. By taking over the Hellenistic educational model we have also swallowed its goals and methodology which are fundamentally cognitive. Our modifications have adapted this somewhat but have left the essential core the same. Conveying knowledge and teaching persons to think are good, but by themselves they are inadequate and imbalanced. In taking over the Hellenistic approach we have duplicated the mistakes of the rabbinic schools and embraced the very approach that Jesus rejected. Rethinking our goals will ultimately mean rethinking our programs and methodology. Academic learning should not be done away with, but our new mentality will mean a transformation of its structure and place in the training process.

If we do not rethink our goals and methodology we will be guided by two factors: the past and the prevailing models around us. These factors should inform our training methods but not conform them.

Use Appropriate Modelers

The most critical factor in leadership training is modeling. When our primary goal is to equip persons for church and outreach ministries, the instructors must be persons who have ministered extensively and effectively in those settings. Bringing together academic learning and real ministry requires that we be much more concerned with the number of years that someone has spent in church ministry than with the number of degrees that they possess. If we disregard this principle we can easily end up placing disfunctional models before potential leaders, persons who tend toward academic teaching because they don't fit in church ministry. Trainees will consciously and unconsciously model the trainers and methods that are put before them. The question is not: "Are we modeling?" We are always modeling. The real question is: "What are we modeling?" This question has radical implications for what instructors and methods we choose.

Another way to keep ministry training and academic learning together is to require instructors to take their sabbaticals in congregational ministry. Another possibility is to employ part- time teachers who are also working in part-time church ministry.

Extend Education and Training Opportunities

How can our schools unite congregational ministry and academic learning? By continuing to extend classes, workshops, and study material to the conference and congregational levels.

Many methods, new and old, can make this possible. Recent developments in electronic and educational technology open new opportunities. Audio and video cassettes and programmed instructional material expand educational alternatives. One of the oldest and simplest methods is the tutorial. It requires only periodic meetings of student and teacher preceded by intensive personal study. This method is almost unheard of in North America but has been used effectively for centuries at Oxford and Cambridge Universities. It can be easily utilized for non- residential education.

Extending studies to persons ministering in the local church must not be seen as an aside to the "primary" task of teaching residential courses and writing scholarly articles. The development of leaders in the local church is the key training task.

Structure Integrative Programs

Our schools have the opportunity to take the lead in developing programs that will fully integrate the elements of effective training: modeling, cognitive learning, intensive ministry, and spiritual formation. While there has been significant progress in this process, some entirely new approaches are needed to intertwine these factors effectively.

The move toward field education and internships is good in our schools but faces definite limitations. Field education is of limited value because it is brief and often largely unsupervised. Internships provide more extended and supervised experiences but they have two drawbacks. First, they come too late in the training process, usually preceded by six years of formal education and followed by only one. Second, while they attempt to unite the cognitive and practical dimensions of ministry they, in fact, leave them basically segmented. Internships simply shove one box of ministry in between two boxes of cognitive learning. Perhaps this is better than nothing but a better integration is possible when they occur simultaneously.

Creative new programs are called for which thoroughly integrate spiritual, relational, skillful and cognitive dimensions. One might be a Master of Ministry degree program. Students in this program would be committed to part-time or near full-time ministry in a local church for at least several years. These learners would be discipled by effective, mature pastors. Those serving small churches would meet regularly with supervising pastors, some might serve in large churches directly under them. These supervising pastors would serve as models providing counsel, instruction, and encouragement in structured yet flexible ways.

Additional cognitive learning could be obtained through inter-term courses, summer sessions, extension classes and correspondence courses. Gift discernment occurring in the congregation could clarify the student's gifts and calling and help guide the direction of his or her studies. Receiving credit for both course work and extensive supervised ministry, the student would be granted a degree after several years or more depending on individual progress toward requirements. Similar programs could be offered on both Bachelor and Associate degree levels. Placing persons in part-time ministries is realistic since many of our congregations are small and this is often where persons begin pastoral ministry. Those called to serve their home congregation would simply stay there with supervision and instruction being made available to them. Programs like this would require careful coordination between schools, conferences, local pastors, and congregations but would offer tremendous opportunities for dynamic pastoral training.

Whatever programs we devise, we must pay careful attention to underlying issues, not just asking, *What* are we teaching?, but also, *How* are we teaching it? The method is the message. We must ask: What is our ultimate goal? Who are we appealing to and excluding by using a particular training model? Are we in tune with New Testament training principles? Are we responding to the real needs of students and churches?

It is encouraging to see the new flexibility in Mennonite leadership training. We must continue to let our mentality and our methods be transformed to integrate fully our equipping efforts.

Following the Chief Shepherd

As pastors, congregations, conferences and schools, we can unite our efforts in dynamic pastoral training as we look to Christ, the Supreme Pastor (1 Pet 5:4). He leads the way in leadership training offering his example, his vision, and his power. He invites us, "Come, follow me!"

ENDNOTES

1. The special relationship of Jesus to the Twelve is clearer in Mark. This can be seen by comparing parallel passages in the Synoptics. The reason for this focus on the Twelve in Mark is explained in the books *Jesus and the Twelve* by Robert Meye and *The Twelve* by Sean Freyne.

2. For a breakdown of Jesus' ministry into areas of involvement see my master's thesis, "Taking the Lead in Leadership Training", Appendix A.

3. A. B. Bruce, *The Training of the Twelve* (N.p.: A. C. Armstrong and Son, 1894; reprint ed. Grand Rapids: Kregel, 1971), 13.

4. Robert E. Coleman, *The Master Plan of Evangelism* (Old Tappan, New Jersey: Fleming H. Revell, 1987), 26-27.

5. James T. Stout, "The Role of the Local Pastor in Equipping Candidates for the Professional Ministry", D. Min. dissertation, Fuller Theological Seminary, 1979, 19-20.

6. A. B. Bruce, *The Training of the Twelve*, 52.

7. For fuller documentation of this assertion, see D. Muller, "Mathetes", in *The New International Dictionary of New Testament Theology* (1975) 1:448-89; and Karl H. Rengstorf, "Didasko", in the *Theological Dictionary of the New Testament* (1964) 2:138-44.

8. Rengstorf, "Didasko", 2:142.

9. Karl H. Rengstorf, "Manthano, Mathetes", in the *Theological Dictionary of the New Testament* (1967) 4:454.

10. T. W. Manson, *The Teaching of Jesus: Studies in its Form and Content* (Cambridge: University Press, 1931), 237-40.

11. Ibid., 239-40.

12. Rengstorf, "Didasko", 2:142.

13. W. Bauder, "Disciple", *The New International Dictionary of New Testament Theology* (1986) 1:488.

14. Herbert V. Klem, *Oral Communication of the Scripture: Insights from African Oral Art* (Pasadena: William Carey, 1982), 83. See also 75-93.

15. Robert E. Coleman, *The Master Plan of Discipleship* (Old Tappan, New Jersey: Fleming H. Revell, 1987), 123.

16. George B. Caird, *The Apostolic Age* (London: Duckworth, 1955), 120.

17. Ibid., 128-9.

18. *Ibid.*, 128.

19. Roland Allen, *Missionary Methods: St. Paul's or Ours?* (Grand Rapids: Eerdmans, 1962), 152.

20. *The Schleitheim Confession*, edited by John H. Yoder (Scottdale, PA: Herald Press, 1977), 13.

21. Leland Harder, *The Pastor-People Partnershiip: The Call and Recall of Pastors From a Believers' Church Perspective* (Elkhart: Institute of Mennonite

Studies, 1983), 23.

22. Arnold Nickel, "Self-Images of the Pastor in the General Conference Mennonite Church", S.T.D. Dissertation, San Francisco Theological Seminary, 1971, 7-8.

23. Harder, *The Pastor-People Partnership, 12.*

24. C. Henry Smith, *Smith's Story of the Mennonites.* 5th edition. Revised and enlarged by Cornelius Krahn. (Newton, KS: Faith and Life Press, 1981), 18.

25. Harder, *The Pastor-People Partnership,* 39.

26. Tim Timmons, "Why Should They Listen to Me?", *Leadership* (Fall, 1985), 90.

27. Paulo Freire, quoted in *Theological Education Today,* 11:4, 11.

28. John Pearce, "St. Augustine on the Education of the Preacher", *Evangelical Review of Theology 5* (October 1981), 293.

29. Arthur Henderson, "Learning the Skills of Leadership", *The Journal of the Christian Brethren Research Fellowship 30* (1980), 67.

30. Robert J. Menges and James E. Dittes, Psychological Studies of Clergymen: Abstracts of Research (New York: Thomas Nelson and Sons, 1965), 51, 53, 67-68. Stout, "The Role of the Local Pastor in Equipping Candidates for the Professional Ministry", 41.

31. F. Ross Kinsler, editor, *Ministry by the People: Theological Education by Extension* (Maryknoll, NY: Orbis, 1983), 15.

32. C. P. Wagner, "Seminaries Ought to be Asking Who as Well as How", Theological Education 10 (Summer 1974), 266-74. F. Ross Kinsler, *The Extension Movement in Theological Education: A Call to the Renewal of the Ministry.* Revised edition (Pasadena, CA: William Carey, 1981), 32-34.

33. Kinsler, *The Extension Movement,* 17.

34. Ibid., 34.

35. Ibid., 15.

36. Ted Ward and Sam Rowen, "The Significance of the Extension Seminary," *Evangelical Missions Quarterly 9* (Fall 1972), 22.

37. Kinsler, *The Extension Movement,* 14-15.

38. Ward and Rowen, "The Significance of the Extension Seminary", 24.

39. Ibid., 27.

40. Robert Michaelson, "The Protestant Ministry in America: 1850 to the Present", *The Ministry in Historical Perspectives,* edited by H. Richard Niebuhr and Daniel Day Williams (New York: Harper, 1956), 274-75.

41. Quoted in Stout, *The Role of the Local Pastor,* 41-42.

42. H. Richard Niebuhr, *The Purpose of the Church and its Ministry* (New York: Harper, 1956), 129-34.

43. Paul Holmer, "Can We Educate Ministers Scientifically?", in Keith R. Bridston and Dwight W. Culver, editors, *The Making of Ministers: Essays on Clergy Training Today* (Minneapolis: Augsburg, 1964), 2-28.

44. Ibid., 26.

45. Ibid., 25.

46. Ray Stedman, "The Impossible Dream: Can Seminaries Deliver?" *Christianity Today* 21 (4 February 1977), 21.

47. Kinsler, *The Extension Movement*, 13.

48. See my article "Different Strands of One Rope: On Using Various Methods of Theological Education", in *Mission Focus* 13 (March 1985), 8.

BIBLIOGRAPHY

"A. A. in Pastoral Ministries." Promotional brochure for Hesston College, n.d.

Allen, Roland. *Missionary Methods: St. Paul's or Ours*. Grand Rapids: Eerdmans, 1962.

Baird, J. A. *Audience Criticism and the Historical Jesus*. Philadephia: Westminster, 1969.

Bauder, W. "Disciple." *Theological Dictionary of the New Testament*. (1986) 1:488.

Bauer, Walter; Arndt, William, F.; and Gingerich, F. Wilbur. *A Greek-English Lexicon of the New Testament and Other Early Christian Literature*. 4th ed. Chicago: University of Chicago Press, 1952.

Bolles, Richard N. *The Three Boxes of Life: And How to Get Out of Them*. Berkeley, CA: Ten Speed Press, 1981.

Bridston, Keith R., and Culver, Dwight W., eds. *The Making of Ministers: Essays on Clergy Training Today*. Minneapolis: Augsburg, 1964.

Bruce, A. B. *The Training of the Twelve*. N.p.: A. C. Armstrong and Son, 1894; reprint ed. Grand Rapids: Kregel, 1971.

Burkholder, J. Lawrence. "Theological Education for the Believers' Church." *Concern* 17 (Feb 1969): 10-32.

Caird, George B. *The Apostolic Age*. London: Duckworth, 1955.

Chao, Jonathan T'ien-en. "Critical Issues in Leadership Training: A Chinese Perspective." In *Mission Focus: Current Issues*, 379-408. Ed. by Wilbert R. Shenk. Scottdale, PA: Herald Press, 1980.

Coleman, Robert E. *The Master Plan of Discipleship*. Old Tappan, NJ: Fleming H. Revell, 1987.

_____, *The Master Plan of Evangelism*. Westwood, NJ: Fleming H. Revell, 1964.

Covell, Ralph R. and Wagner, C. Peter. *An Extension Seminary Primer*. South Pasadena, CA: William Carey, 1971.

Detweiler, Richard C. and Miller, Marlin E. "A Proposed Model for Mennonite Church Ministry and Leadership Training." November 6, 1981. Mimeographed.

Dyck, Cornelius J., ed. *An Introduction to Mennonite History*. Scottdale, PA: Herald Press, 1981.

Egli, Jim. "Different Strands of One Rope: On Using Various Methods of Theological Education." *Mission Focus* 13 (March 1985): 8.

Freyne, Sean. *The Twelve Disciples and Apostles: A Study in the Theology of the First Three Gospels*. London: Sheed and Ward, 1968.

Friesen, Jacob T. and Poettcker, Henry. "General Conference Mennonite Church Ministry and Leadership Training." March 29, 1982. Revised May 25, 1982. Mimeographed.

Harder, Leland. *The Pastor-People Partnership: The Call and Recall of Pastors from a Believers' Church Perspective*. Elkhart: Institute of Mennonite Studies, 1983.

Henderson, Arthur. "Learning the Skills of Leadership." *The Journal of the Christian Brethren Research Fellowship* 30 (1980): 65-72.

The Holy Bible: New International Version. Grand Rapids: Zondervan, 1978.

Kinsler, F. Ross. *The Extension Movement in Theological Education: A Call to the Renewal of the Ministry*. Revised ed. Pasadena, CA: William Carey, 1981.

_____, ed. *Ministry by the People: Theological Education by Extension*. Maryknoll, NY: Orbis, 1983.

Klem, Herbert V. *Oral Communication of the Scripture: Insights from African Oral Art*. Pasadena: William Carey, 1982.

Krahn, Cornelius. "Ministry: German." *Mennonite Encyclopedia* (1957) 3:701-3.

Lohse, Eduard. "Rabbi, rabbouni." *Theological Dictionary of the New Testament* (1968) 6:961-65.

MacDonald, Gordon. "Some Questions Seminaries Must Face." *Evangelical Newsletter* 4 (June 17, 1977): 4.

Manson, T. W. *The Teaching of Jesus: Studies in Its Form and Content.* Cambridge: University Press, 1931.

Menges, Robert J. and Dittes, James E. *Psychological Studies of Clergymen: Abstracts of Research.* New York: Thomas Nelson and Sons, 1965.

Meye, R. P. *Jesus and the Twelve: Discipleship and Revelation in Mark's Gospel.* Grand Rapids: Eerdmans, 1968.

Muller, D. "Mathetes." *The New International Dictionary of New Testament Theology* (1975) 1:483.

Neff, Christian; Bender, H. S.; and van der Zijpp, N. "Call to the Ministry." *Mennonite Encyclopedia* (1957) 3:704-7.

Nickel, Arnold. "Self-Images of the Pastor in the General Conference Mennonite Church." S.T.D. dissertation, San Francisco Theological Seminary, 1971.

Niebuhr, H. Richard. *The Purpose of the Church and Its Ministry.* New York: Harper and Brothers, 1956.

Pearce, John. "St. Augustine on the Education of the Preacher." *Evangelical Review of Theology* 5 (October 1981): 287-93.

Rengstorf, Karl H. "Didasko." *Theological Dictionary of the New Testament* (1964) 2:135-68.

_____. "Manthano, mathetes." *Theological Dictionary of the New Testament* (1967) 4:390-461.

Smith, C. Henry. *Smith's Story of the Mennonites.* 5th ed. Revised and enlarged by Cornelius Krahn. Newton, KS: Faith and Life

Press, 1981.

Smith, Willard H. *Mennonites in Illinois*. Studies in Anabaptist and Mennonite History, 24. Scottdale, PA: Herald Press, 1983.

Stedman, Ray. "The Impossible Dream: Can Seminaries Deliver?" *Christianity Today* 21 (4 February 1977): 21.

Stout, James T. "The Role of the Local Pastor in Equipping Candidates for the Professional Ministry." D.Min. dissertation, Fuller Theological Seminary, 1979.

Timmons, Tim. "Why Should They Listen to Me?" *Leadership* (Fall 1985):90.

van der Zijpp, N. "Ministry: Netherlands." *Mennonite Encyclopedia* (1957) 3:699-701.

Wagner, C. Peter. "Seminaries Ought to Be Asking Who as Well as How." *Theological Education* 10 (Summer 1974): 266-74.

Ward, Ted and Rowen, Sam. "The Significance of the Extension Seminary." *Evangelical Missions Quarterly* 9 (Fall 1972): 17-27.

Yoder, John H. ed. *The Schleitheim Confession*. Scottdale, PA: Herald Press, 1977.

Chapter 3
Responses

Multiple Ways of Learning

Lois Barrett

Theological education happens--and should happen--on many different levels. It happens in graduate seminaries, in undergraduate colleges, in Bible colleges and Bible schools, in conference-based programs, in the worship and education programs of local congregations. Moreover, theological education is intended for people serving in a variety of contexts. The two papers published here reflect the variety of theological education opportunities that are developing.

The present variety seems new because for the last few decades, graduate seminaries have been seen as the preferred setting for the training of pastors, modified by Clinical Pastoral Education, Congregationally Supervised Pastoral Education, internships, urban pastoral training programs, and so forth. This has not always been the case, however. Fifty years ago, many Mennonite communities had winter Bible schools. Ministers had apprenticed or supervised relationships with elders/bishops/overseers. (The terminology was different depending on one's conference.) Mennonite graduate seminary training in North America began in 1914 with the Mennonite (later Witmarsum) Seminary--inter-Mennonite in concept but supported primarily by the General Conference Mennonites and the Central Conference of Mennonites. The Mennonite Church entered graduate theological education in 1946, at about the time the General Conference made a fresh start with a new seminary.

Since that time, the percentage of seminary-trained pastors among Mennonite congregations has risen, along with the rise in educational level of the rest of the members of the congregations and of North Americans in general. As of 1989, the percentages were even higher than the 1981 figures which Paul Zehr quotes in his article. Among full-time Mennonite Church (MC) pastors in 1989, 64 percent had had at least some seminary education. Forty percent had graduated from seminary. In the General Conference Mennonite Church (GC) in 1989, the figures were even higher. Eighty-five percent of full-time pastors had at least some seminary education, and 65 percent had graduated.[1]

At the same time, many pastors and church leaders have had

little theological training beyond the local congregation. Some of them may find it difficult in mid-life to uproot family and move to a seminary campus. The question is how best to meet the theological education needs of Mennonite pastors and churches.

Paul M. Zehr's article is a description of the Conference-Based Pastoral Education program in Lancaster Mennonite Conference, a context in which fewer pastors have seminary training than in some other areas of the church.

The article reflects some years of careful thinking, exploration, and experimentation with a new model of theological education which   integrates being, knowing, doing, and attitudes. There is a clear target audience and a model of pastoral ministry: the pastor as equipper of the saints for the work of ministry.

Jim Egli's paper, on the other hand, is not so much description as prescription, an argument for more experience-based learning in the context of the local congregation. His emphasis is on doing--as opposed to knowing. Although Egli is careful not to advocate doing away with cognitive learning entirely, it clearly has a subordinate place in his proposal.

However, there is a problem with his using Jesus and Paul as models for theological education for twentieth-century pastors. As Egli notes, Jesus sat down and taught in a formal sense, as well as modeling, demonstrating, and giving the disciples practical experience. Yet, when Egli comes to drawing conclusions, the implications of Jesus' formal teachings are ignored.

Secondly, the pastoral role as it has developed in the modern age has no exact parallels in Jesus or in the New Testament church. Egli does not advocate that all pastors travel around the countryside with a band of disciples as Jesus did, or travel around the world from congregation to congregation as Paul did. The elder/bishop/presbyter role in the New Testament church was one of many leadership roles in the church; it is not identical with the modern pastoral role. Most Mennonite churches have structured themselves differently from the New Testament congregations. Are we to train pastors for the roles and congregations that are, or restructure our congregations? We need to learn from the New Testament church, and at the same time be careful about reading our own institutional roles into the New Testament.

The solution to an overemphasis on cognitive learning is not to ignore it or throw it out, but to integrate it. The teaching of Jesus in John 14:21-23 is helpful here:

"They who have my commandments and keep them are those who love me; and those who love me will be loved by my

Father, and I will love them and reveal myself to them."
Judas (not Iscariot) said to him, "Lord, how is it that you will
reveal yourself to us, and not to the world?" Jesus answered
him, "Those who love me will keep my word, and my Father
will love them, and we will come to them and make our home
with them."

In other words, the secret of knowing, and knowing Jesus, is
doing, keeping his word. Knowing and doing are bound up together.
Depending upon our own learning style, we tend to prefer different
contexts of learning.

One of the most helpful models for me in understanding different ways of learning has been the 4Mat System of Bernice
McCarthy.[2] Her learning circle is divided into quadrants. In the
first quadrant are the concrete, reflective learners. Their main question is, Why? Why is this important? Why are we doing this? They
want to reflect on their experience. They want reasons.

In the second quadrant are the abstract, reflective learners,
whose question is, What? That is the question which most traditional academic learning has tried to answer. They want to know
facts and skills. But they are also good at developing models and
theories. They usually like traditional schooling.

Third-quadrant learners are abstract, active learners. They ask,
How? How could we do this? They get busy developing a plan of
action, engineering a program. How does this apply to life? How
could we put this theory/model/idea into practice?

In the fourth quadrant are the concrete, active learners who
ask, What if? What if we did it this way? Or actually they prefer to
talk about it as little as possible. They say, "Let's just do it." They
learn by doing, and they learn by teaching it to others.

The most helpful learning processes include all four types.
True, the academic learning that most of us have received, from
about the fourth grade on, is heavy on the What? It is abstract and
reflective. But we do not help ourselves by simply switching our
overemphasis to concrete, active learning. Each of us, no matter
what our learning style, benefits from all four ways of teaching.

All four types can happen in structured educational programs,
depending on the course. At a minimum, an instructor can spend
some time asking, Why is it important to study this? What is the
content of this course? How can you plan to use this knowledge in
your ministry? Can we find a way for you to practice doing this or
teaching this?

Implications for theological education: (1) There is a need to
educate all four types of learners, without elevating one learning

style over another, or putting down those who do not have our preferred learning style. We would not appreciate a pastor who studied much and carefully, but never preached--nor a pastor who never studied or planned, but simply spoke from the top of the head.

(2) There is a place for centralized graduate (or undergraduate) theological education. Its advantages are the larger community of study, the extensive library resources, its specialized teachers. It can benefit both people who go three years straight for a master of divinity degree and those who dip in several times on sabbaticals or interterms.

(3) Decentralized models of theological education are becoming increasingly important--for the two-career family, mid-life career changers, people in shared ministry situations or bi-vocational ministry, people testing the possibilities for ministry, who may later go on to a centralized theological institution, and pastors seeking continuing education.

(4) Apprenticeships, an ancient form of learning, are still important, both as a part of formal education and subsequent to it. Apprenticeships can be holistic as well; the best apprenticeships involve reflection, study, and planning as well as just doing.

Mennonites, who have long understood the connection between knowing and doing, the inseparability of theology and ethics, can be pioneers in new models of education. If we try only to know and to study, we will not accomplish much in sharing Christ's message in the church and in the world. If we try only to do, we will be like Washington Irving's headless horseman who rode off madly in all directions. It does not help for concrete, active learners and abstract, reflective learners to throw stones at each other.

Instead, we need to develop models of theological education that speak to all four types of learners and that challenge all learners to go beyond the learning style with which they are comfortable, to understand the wholeness of the faith and develop holistic ways of passing on that faith to others.

ENDNOTES

1. Ministerial Leadership Services office, Newton, Kansas.
2. Bernice McCarthy, *The 4Mat System: Teaching to Learning Styles with Right/Left Mode Techniques*, 2nd ed. (Oak Brook, Ill.: Excel, 1981).

Charting Direction: Some Change in the Status Quo or a Radical Change?

Harold E. Bauman

Paul M. Zehr in "A Curriculum Guide for Mennonite Conference-Based Pastoral Education" seeks to answer the question: Who will train the many bivocational pastors who have not attended seminaries and what kind of training program is needed?

Zehr sees four areas of concern in designing a training program for effective pastoral ministry: what the pastor must *be, know, do,* and what *attitudes* the pastor must have in ministry.

Four major studies are used by Zehr as the background basis for the proposed curriculum. The first is a biblical theological study, focusing primarily on Ephesians 4:7-16. The key idea is that the pastoral gift is to equip members for mission and service and that this requires a major change in how pastors are educated. The change is not indicated at this point.

The second background study makes use of the Mennonite Board of Education statement on a philosophy of education (1971) and the statement of the Associated Mennonite Biblical Seminaries on a philosophy of Theological Education in the Free Church Tradition (1971). Zehr also reviews the emphases of the Anabaptists in regard to leaders as well as those of several Mennonite leaders in the twentieth century. He concludes with sixteen summary statements on a Mennonite philosophy of pastoral education. Surprisingly I found no statement explicitly focusing on training pastors to have skills to equip members for their ministry.

The third background study is of extension programs in theological education. After listing a number of deficiencies of the western seminary models of education, Zehr describes the beginning of theological education by extension and its rapid growth. A number of advantages of the approach of taking education to the pastors rather than taking the pastors to the seminary are listed. Eight implications are drawn for conference-based pastoral education.

The fourth background study is on experience-based learning, commonly called Clinical Pastoral Education (CPE). Zehr overviews the development of CPE from its beginning in 1925, its emphases and some problems that continue to plague the movement. This section is concluded with a number of observations from parish-based CPE programs which can inform conference-based pastoral training.

Zehr then presents a curriculum guide which is recommended

for training bivocational pastors. He begins by presenting an educational philosophy including *approach* which assesses the needs of each student; *scope* which combines classrooms, semidecentralized settings and congregation-based Supervised Pastoral Education (SPE) for pastors and key lay leaders; *content* which includes spiritual formation, knowledge of scriptures, church history and theology, development of skills for pastoral ministry, and creation of positive attitudes toward ministry; *context* which keeps the student functioning in a congregation; *faculty* who are experienced in pastoral ministry; and *methodology* which integrates classroom learnings with learnings gained by experience in ministry and which includes SPE after completion of a foundation studies program.

Ten educational objectives follow, indicating the outcomes desired as the result of the program. The proposed Conference-Based Pastoral Education curriculum follows with three major components: a Foundation Studies Program, Supervised Pastoral Education, and Continuing Education. Two tracks are offered in the Foundation Studies Program: a day track which takes two years to complete and an evening track which takes four years. A listing of the courses for each track is presented and followed by a brief description of each of the required courses and some elective courses.

The second component--Supervised Pastoral Education--is described and a course syllabus used September-December, 1986 is included.

Continuing education, the third component, consists of two courses each year, one in the autumn and the other in the winter, for pastors and key lay leaders. The courses are offered on ten consecutive Thursday evenings. A syllabus on themes in Old Testament theology is included as an example course.

The total document concludes with a bibliography of the works used in developing the manuscript.

The manuscript reflects the careful study of the author and the years of experience through his involvement in the various educational efforts of the Lancaster Conference. The manuscript reflects good solid work which moves in the direction of training congregational leaders in the Believers' Church model.

The Lancaster Conference is the largest in the Mennonite Church and most of the congregations are within a reasonable driving distance of a teaching center. Two other conferences are in close proximity and the three conferences have cooperated in the continuing education model for some years. Many conferences in the Mennonite Church are much more widely scattered. Several considerations result: more travel expense for the teaching staff and the students and less income to pay for the program in view of fewer students and fewer supporting congregations. These conferences will need to discover plans which fit their settings, making adaptations as needed.

In the biblical study Zehr places a great deal of emphasis on the fact that the gifts named in Ephesians 4:11 are to equip the members for their ministry. His writing which follows prompts some questions.

First, why choose only the pastor-teacher as the one who needs special training? Zehr writes that "Paul identifies apostles, prophets, evangelists, pastors and teachers." He then focuses on their task given in 4:12 and concludes, "In short, the function of the pastoral gift is to equip the members for mission and service." I am wondering if only the pastoral gift does equipping in the congregation. "Pastor-teacher" is one way of translating the words of Paul. Are there no teachers at the congregational leadership level to be trained? Are none of the apostles, prophets, evangelists included in the congregational leadership? Do they function only in inter-congregational ministry? Who trains them? One could make a case that at least the prophets and evangelists are part of congregational leadership.

A second question raises the issue of the nature of congregational leadership. Let us look at this issue through two windows. Zehr writes that both the Foundation Studies Program and Continuing Education are to train pastors and key lay leaders. We are not told the function of the key lay leaders--their work and how they relate to the work of the pastor. In Acts and Paul's pastoral epistles, congregational leaders are called "elders." Are they all pastors (a term which does not occur in those books)? In 1 Timothy 5:17 it appears there is a plurality of elders and a diversity of gifts within them. Thus one window on congregational leadership is its plurality and its diversity of gifts. To speak primarily of training pastors and key lay leaders is a direction to be affirmed in contrast to the usual Protestant model; does it, however, speak clearly enough to training a plural leadership in the Believers' Church?

A second window to look at the nature of congregational leadership is through the New Testament understanding of spiritual gifts. Paul writes in I Corinthians 12:11 that the Spirit allots to each one individually as the Spirit chooses, and in 12:29-30 that no one receives all the gifts. The educational objectives are written to apply to each student. Objective 5 reads, "Enhance the skills for ministry including preaching, administration, teaching, pastoral care, and evangelism." (Where is the equipping of members for ministry?) This appears to assume each student (pastor?) will be able to do all of these ministries. It is my understanding of the New Testament teaching on spiritual gifts that no one individual will have all of these gifts; it will take plural leadership for all the gifts to be present. To lay the expectation on students that "pastoral training" will equip them in all these areas will continue producing frustrated pastors and disappointed congregations. We are continuing a Protestant model of ministry, not a Believers' Church one.

A third question related to congregational leadership focusing on the primary task of equipping members for their ministry within and outside the body is where this is reflected in the required courses. The course on "Congregational Evangelism in the Believers' Church" includes equipping members for evangelism and service. Equipping members is not apparent in the other courses, though the other courses help persons with background needed to give the broad base for members in such training. However, how is the translation made for congregational leaders to equip members to use their spiritual gifts in ministry? How are spiritual gifts discerned and released? Where do members get training, for example, in the wise use of the gifts of knowledge, wisdom, mercy, etc. What are some training methods congregational leaders can use? A required course on "Releasing and Training Members for Ministry" is strongly indicated to follow through on the basic thrust of the biblical study.

Two further observations. Much is made of what the pastor must be and the need for spiritual formation. I affirm the required course on Spiritual Formation and Spiritual Disciplines. The inclusion of an educational objective explicitly for this area (and early in the list) could help underscore the importance of this area.

The second observation is the need for a required course on "Authority, Decision Making, and Conflict Resolution in the Believers' Church." What is authority? Who makes major decisions in congregational life? How can good communication and decision making processes be developed? When differences arise, how can they be resolved in positive ways? What are the dynamics of conflict in congregational life? Such a course is needed by all congregational leaders.

Paul Zehr's proposals point good directions: pastors and key leaders are trained by extension; students continue to function in their congregations; experience, teaching, and reflection are integrated; and supervised experience is offered (after completing the basic studies). The proposals are informed by current seminary models, depart from them in the good directions just noted, yet the long familiarity with Protestant seminary models leaves its imprint: primary focus on the classroom and primary focus on the pastor.

A more radical proposal for leadership training is "Leadership Training for the Church of the Future" by James Egli. His purpose is to focus on *how* to train leaders, rather than on the *what* or content of the training. His thesis is that effective leadership training is not primarily acquiring information and learning how to think theologically, but more a matter of learning how to relate to God and to others.

The growth in relationships and relational skills involves several crucial elements: a deep reliance on God through prayer, an apprentice relationship with a local pastor or leader, the support of other believers, cognitive learning and actual involvement in ministry. To be effective these elements must be intertwined at each point in the equipping process.

Egli examines the leadership training style of Jesus, asserting that Jesus gave top priority to leadership training. In the gospel of Mark, Egli holds that the record of Jesus' ministry to the public and his disciples is divided about equally. Furthermore, Jesus trained leaders at different levels. The disciples observed his ministry to the public. Jesus also spent time with the Twelve. Within the Twelve was the group of three.

The methods Jesus used in training include: leading the disciples into a close relationship with himself, teaching by demonstration, involving the disciples in actual ministry to develop the skills needed for future leadership and service, and modeling and teaching a life of prayer as crucial to one's ministry.

Egli notes that Jesus rejected the established educational pattern in the Rabbinic system which looks surprisingly like the academic, residential model we have embraced today. The Rabbinic and current models are academically focused which is foreign to the Hebraic focus on the whole person. Egli holds that Jesus affirmed the role and calling of the Christian scholar, though he used a different method for leadership training. Egli asks whether we have the courage to lay aside respected and established training patterns to use more dynamic methods of leadership training.

In concluding the study of the training Jesus gave the Twelve, Egli affirms that equipping for ministry required empowering by the Spirit of God. Both the initial and ongoing filling of the Spirit must be emphasized.

Egli then moves to Paul and notes that he rejected the Rabbinic pattern of education, used in-service training, prayer and fasting and the relational learning process. Egli states that Paul had three distinctive emphases: identification with others, modeling as a way of training, and showing confidence in others. The heart of successful training happens through sharing and ministry in which fellowship with God can be modeled and priorities and skills demonstrated.

After reviewing Anabaptist leadership patterns, the plural ministry through the centuries, and the move to one trained pastor in this century, Egli proposes three New Testament principles to guide our leadership training.

The first principle is that the trainers must be successful, competent pastors, not academic professors, who establish mentor relationships with the learners.

The second principle is that the setting is actual ministry rather than the classroom setting. In this setting learners gain the skills they need in ministry; the medium is the message.

The third principle is that the goals in the New Testament were relational rather than informational. The academic model teaches persons *to know* rather than to be able to relate to God and those around.

Egli reports his research on factors involved in persons experiencing a call to ministry. Practical experience in ministry and relation to a pastor were the factors mentioned most often.

Egli then reviews current trends in theological education and the voices calling for more practical experience in ministry during the training period. He notes that Mennonite seminaries are encouraging more practical experience, though Egli calls these efforts appendages to the academic model.

In his final chapter, Egli develops a strategy for leadership training. For both theological and educational reasons the key elements for equipping leaders--modeling, spiritual formation, practical experience, cognitive learning and personal interaction--must be integrated into ministry relationships.

Pastors are the vital link in leadership training. Pastors are not doing leadership training because they were not trained that way themselves. Congregations need to free pastors to give more time to leadership training. Conferences can train pastors on how to do leadership training.

Egli calls our training institutions to develop a new mindset by setting relational goals in training. Faculty should be persons with a number of years in ministry. Another option is persons who are part-time in ministry and part-time teaching. More classes by extension are needed. More settings are needed where learners are apprenticed to experienced pastors.

Egli's final call is to follow Jesus, the Supreme Pastor, in his leadership training example.

Egli develops a very cogent case to shift the *primary* focus in leadership training from *what is taught* to *how it is taught*. He gives a number of practical suggestions to move in that direction. His call for congregationally-based leadership training, supplemented by courses and seminars could be used as the main approach in conference-based training. The courses could supplement the supervised training at every level, not just after the foundation courses are completed.

The shift to congregationally-based leadership training will not come easily. The redirection of funds, finding successful experienced pastors and training them in supervision, and finding instructors with a number of years of successful pastoral ministry will take some time.

The vision is presented. The New Testament call is clear enough to be heeded. Hopefully it will be.

A Theological Framework Gives Foundation and Stability for Ministry

Richard C. Detweiler

Thanks to Paul Zehr and Jim Egli for providing handles to get hold of the foremost need for the education and training of persons in and for church leadership. I use the terms, "education" and "training" as different though complementary approaches to the development of ministerial leaders. Zehr's approach indicates greater attention to theological understanding and the implications thereof for ministry and for which the idea of education is appropriate, although he as well as Egli also uses freely the term, training, and both endorse TEE as a viable educational/training approach. Zehr also proposes CPE and SPE as important means of pastoral formation. Egli's thesis is focused more on experiential hands-on preparation for leadership which is rightly referred to as training. Both education and training can be considered valid concepts of pastoral formation.

I can affirm Zehr's emphasis on the congregational paradigm rather than a clerical paradigm for pastoral education as well as the pastor-teacher-equipper concept of ministry. I can likewise support Egli's attention to the discipling method of in-service training. The integration of Zehr's more theologically oriented approach and subsequent curriculum with Egli's Jesus-style training of disciples "on the way" would be a good program. I recognize that both writers are indeed attempting that combination in their own respective ways, so it may be a matter of which inclination forms the basic orientation for pastoral development.

Let me comment on several directions indicated by both Zehr and Egli.

The Congregational Context

The congregational context for education that both papers endorse is a viable setting. However, it should not be too quickly assumed that an extended period away from one's familiar living and serving environment is only a disadvantage. The opportunity to focus study and reflection in a more concentrated and sustained way, the new perspectives discovered in a different community, the broadening of church and personal relationships, the accessibility of resources, especially library, the experience of self and spouse and family socialization in new surroundings all have potentially positive benefits. Admittedly, there are the problems of academic immersion, distance from in-depth involvement in congregational life, and family adjustment stresses including financial anxieties, spouse employment and children's schooling.

Pastoral formation in the congregational context often assumes the trainee is continuing to prepare to function on his or her own home turf which is not necessarily the best context nor automatic match. The training of Jesus' disciples took place away from home, sometimes even in hostile environs, and their further ministry was not in their original locality.

Having said the above, it is still a valid point that persons who are called in their respective congregations are already known for their character and gifts and can be authentically discerned and affirmed for leadership. Congregations should be the locus for ministerial calling. But that does not necessarily mean that the calling, therefore, is to be exercised in one's home congregation. We should be preserving and advocating the concept of congregational calling and providing for the training of persons, but recognize the outcome may be the ministry of those persons being fulfilled elsewhere as a reciprocal service with other congregations who are doing the same.

Theological Undergirdings of Pastoral Formation

Theological theorems can be sterile in producing effective ministry. However, theological assumptions inevitably inform education/training content and methodology. A developmental need of many good pastors is to understand the theological premises and implications by which they are operating. A theological framework gives foundation and stability for ministry and allows for flexibility and innovation without losing one's bearings in fads and one-dimensional instant success methodologies. Theological depth also contributes to an Anabaptist/Mennonite orientation for leadership. The caution of hands-on training is a tempting reliance on "how to do" without a sufficiently commensurate "how to know and be." Both Egli and Zehr urge the integration of knowing, being and doing. The relevancy of theological education is not always immediately apparent, but in the long-term role of the church minister, persons discover they are drawing on theological understandings more than they anticipated they would do. Even our relationships in ministry are formulated by our theological responses to our sociological situations. Closely related also is that one's view of the church (ecclesiology) forms one's view of the role of leadership which in turn influences one's view of education/training. A church leader's self-perception and way of relating to others in ministry are theological developments for they express his or her way of experiencing God and interpreting biblical doctrines.

Priesthood of Believers

While the New Testament teachings and Anabaptist applications thereof take seriously the priesthood of all believers as including all members being called to ministry, one should not unduly strain to minimize the calling of persons to specific leadership roles with designated authority. Anabaptist/Mennonite designated roles of church leadership are seen to be exercised *among*, not *to* (Roman Catholic) nor *for* (general Protestant) the congregation. However, servant leadership should not imply passive subservience nor the abandonment of leading, but rather the assertion of leadership ministry in a servant or serving style. The pastoral formation should look toward creating both a "going before" initiative and the facilitating and equipping of others for a participatory "going along." This view commends a plural ministry but recognizes that a pluralistic system needs persons called both to exercise leadership and to model and prepare persons for it.

Stages and Diversity of Leadership

Pastoral formation calls for educational training suited to experience levels, from exploratory gift discernment, to apprenticeship, to leader responsibility, to refurbishing, to new forms or settings of ministry and to "active retirement" such as interim pastoring. In other words, we might consider supplementing generic leadership education/training with more definitive focus and in-depth concentration than what is now available, even though our training centers have curriculum tracks. Furthermore, we should give more attention to specific need situations such as, for example, ministers in transition.

Further Thoughts

To again reiterate affirmation for the work of Egli and Zehr in identifying the essential elements in enabling pastoral formation, I would urge us all in pastoral, administrative or institutional leadership not only to recognize the educational training need for developing church leadership, but to become more coordinately intentional in providing for the same with theological undergirding, experiential opportunities and contemporary relevance.

Such education/training will be expressed in some curricular form. Egli's thesis leaves us with the further need to formulate more specific content of what is to be taught. Zehr prescribes curriculum content which is finally necessary even in the discipling mode of training. For example, I heartily agree with the need to grow in the experience of prayer, but what concept of prayer, its anticipation, its applications, its ministry to others forms the minister's practice? If the "established educational pattern is rejected", what then constitutes the substance and measurement of education/training? The response may be that I have missed the point that the medium becomes both the person and practice message. But given the premise that most of us are not Jesus, the intentionality of education/training requires that the message needs to be more than the training medium.

That leads to another consideration pertaining to Zehr's curriculum. It seems strange that, given our definition of church leadership as including the equipping of others, we do not seem to provide training for that aspect of ministry. Should there not be some form of training for equippers to develop others competently for leadership? To reiterate, the most viable principle of education/training by which to develop persons for church leadership may be to keep together and integrate those hyphenated terms as methodology and content are formulated. This may also speak to the point not addressed by either paper directly, namely, how to bring together the concepts of professional competence and Spirit-led and gifted calling. Hopefully the two are not antithetical, but rather two sides of the same coin of ministerial authenticity in which "all is of God".

In recent years, one of the Mennonite Church efforts to encourage and facilitate a more coordinated and wholistic church leadership education/training has been the forming of the Theological Education Committee by the Mennonite Board of Education which works closely also with the Theological Education Group of the General Conference Mennonite Church. The purpose is to assess pastoral training needs, to identify current provisions for the same, and to evaluate how the educational programs of our institutional training centers can be integrated with conference-based and extension forms of church leadership development.

Five Mentoring Roles

Ralph A. Lebold

What will be the shape of pastoral education programs in the next decade? This question surfaces with full force as both writers challenge current patterns of pastoral education and make proposals for change. The writers pose a serious challenge to the institutional/academic model of preparing pastors for ministry. Zehr begins with a utilitarian approach where he indicates that the seminaries educate approximately 25% of the Mennonite Church pastors. He asks, "Who will train the many bivocational pastors who have not attended seminary?" Egli examines the pattern of Jesus and Paul concluding that both used an action/reflection mode where involvement in ministry, modeling and nurturing a deeper relationship with God were primary ingredients in training disciples/leaders.

The response to these educational proposals will focus on five areas - students, context, content, methodology and mentors. At the outset, both writers are affirmed for their readiness to articulate visions and programs for pastoral education. The tone of the materials is one of support for the denomination in searching for additional ways to respond to the urgent need to train pastors. Their critique of the current models sets the stage for a healthy discussion.

1. The Student Group

Zehr, who works within a Conference-based Theological Education structure, focuses his primary interests on persons serving in leadership roles without previous formal training, persons with training wanting to do continuing education, and persons who want to test their interest and gifts for ministry. Egli appears to be less clear in his focus. One the one hand, he discusses ministerial training (ch.6) but in reality he appears to be working with an apprenticeship model where persons can test their call to ministry and where persons (lay and ordained) can gain some ministry experience in the context of the congregation. He draws heavily on concepts from Theological Education by Extension (TEE). Both writers demonstrate limitations and promise in their proposals. Zehr's proposal is shaped substantially by the fact that the Lancaster Conference continues to ordain a major portion of its pastors directly out of the congregation. Many conferences do not follow this pattern and have significantly larger numbers of pastors with seminary education. The strength of the proposal is that it takes seriously the needs of persons who are in ministry already.

Egli's student group are members of the congregation discerned to have potential to be pastors or lay leaders. It is not clear whether he envisions this as a model for every congregation or whether he sees selected congregations as teaching congregations offering apprenticeship opportunities for prospective leaders. Would he welcome students from other congregations? The strength of this proposal lies in the emphasis on discerning and calling persons to the vocation of ministry and in equipping lay leaders. In this sense these programs provide a potential personnel resource for seminaries engaged in a more intensive educational process.

The reality is that there are many persons who are not in ministry or directly connected to their congregation of origin who are seeking training as preparation for ministry. The two proposals do not address directly this group of people. Zehr addresses the needs of a particular group of persons - pastors in ministry. Egli focuses on congregational members who want to test their call to ministry and lay persons who need training for their leadership roles.

2. Context

The significant element in both proposals is that the congregation becomes the central context for equipping persons for ministry. In promoting the TEE model, Egli critiques traditional ministerial training which "required persons to leave their natural setting and church relationships in order to enroll in a residential school. After years of costly academic training the persons are then artificially plugged back into the church with a new role and a new status." The assumptions inherent in this critique clearly fit third world realities, some North American minority groups (e.g., Hispanics, Blacks), and possibly rural Mennonite churches which have elements of the traditional lay ministry in their background. Given the professional understanding of ministry which is characteristic of an increasing number of conferences and congregations, I doubt whether the problem he identifies is as serious as he suggests.

Zehr assumes the congregational context for other reasons. As noted in the previous section, this is where the pastoral students are located who form his training group. Also, in his emphasis on experience-based learning, the congregation is essential as an educational context. Zehr does incorporate the traditional classroom model as one element in the equipping process but he never loses sight of the importance of the congregation.

Both Egli and Zehr have captured an important ingredient in pastoral formation and in equipping persons for ministry. The context is a significant factor in shaping pastoral identity, in testing aptitude and skills for ministry as well as providing an appropriate data base for the action/reflection model of learning. Seminaries will need to take the congregational context seriously in the equipping of persons for ministry in the church if they wish to address the Egli/Zehr concerns.

Conversely, Egli is not clear on the role of the institution in his educational model. Zehr assumes an institutional resource from which to draw his teaching faculty. The question is whether decentralized programs can function in a viable form without a solid, central educational base. I suspect both writers would affirm the need for the central base for a variety of reasons but at least in Egli's proposal this fact is not clear.

3. Content

Both Zehr and Egli spell out a program to educate for ministry. Zehr identifies spiritual formation, a solid knowledge base, skills for pastoral ministry and the development of positive attitudes toward the Christian ministry as ingredients in the equipping process. He proposes a series of courses to promote cognitive learning and Congregationally Supervised Pastoral Education (CSPE) to achieve the remaining goals. Egli, on the other hand, puts less stress on content learning and focuses an integrative approach combining cognitive input, field experiences and seminars where persons are encouraged to "make direct application of new knowledge to experience."

These proposals raise the question as to what is involved in preparing persons for ministry in the church. At the content level we have put, historically, a heavy emphasis on cognitive learning with an appropriate knowledge base as the essential element in pastoral education. The faculty debates around curriculum development have centered on discipline balance while constituencies have pushed for relevance and knowledge related to contemporary issues.

Both proposals begin to push us in the right direction in relation to content. A knowledge base is important, not only as a basis for preaching and teaching, but serve as background for creating strong, effective pastoral leaders. Other goals, such as stressing personal formation, the development of ministry expertise and leadership skills, are also significant for the equipping task. The following diagram may help to envision the scope of the pastoral education task.

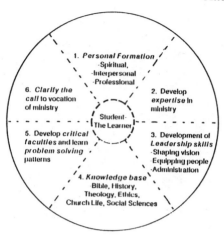

Units 1-4 can be programmed through courses and ministry experiences. Units 5-6 are by-products of the educational experience. Except for unit 5, both proposals incorporate the tasks identified in the other units as significant elements for the educational process.

4. Methodology

Zehr's model seeks to integrate "cognitive learnings through a Foundation Studies Program with learnings gained in the practice of ministry." As noted in the content section, Egli promotes an interactive model with the seminar as the connecting link between ideas and experience. These models assume congregational life and work as the base from which the ministry data comes.

These proposals contain more than procedural suggestions for equipping leaders. They challenge some fundamental assumptions about the nature of education. Zehr argues for a shift from a Hellenistic view of education to a Hebraic one which "emphasizes covenant community...." Egli begins with an examination of the approaches of Jesus and Paul and uses these persons as models for his approach. Both challenge the academic model, the acquisition of knowledge, as being the primary focus for pastoral education. Modern day seminaries, they charge, have bought heavily into these assumptions.

I concur with their critique and call for alternate models for training pastors. N. Keith Clifford[1] in a recent article has written an insightful piece which describes and critiques theological education in Canada. He says,

The two most profound structural changes in theological education in the last three decades have been the formation of university departments of religious studies and the ecumenical clustering of theological colleges in major university centers.(1)

In discussing the first change he notes its profound effect on the English-speaking seminaries in Canada. He says,

Therefore, insofar as the seminaries are engaged in graduate theological education and determined to incorporate into their research and publication the standards which have been set for the academic study of religion, they are perceived to be responding more to the demands of the university and less to the needs of the churches. Such a structural change, therefore, has had profound implications for the relationship between the theological colleges and the church.(4)

Assuming that Clifford's assessment has validity and assuming that this influence, to a greater or lesser extent, is also true for the USA, then we must ask whether the Mennonite seminaries have also been influenced by these trends. Increasing numbers of seminary professors are being educated in Departments of Religion at secular universities and in mainline seminaries which have adopted the graduate school model of education. How do these educational experiences influence the assumptions of the persons who shape seminary education programs? Rethinking our educational methodologies calls for a careful examination of educational philosophies. What would it mean for content and methodology if Zehr's Hebraic philosophy of education was adopted as an approach to equipping pastors for ministry?

A key ingredient in the educational methodology in both proposals is an action/reflection model of learning with supervision as a central function. This emphasis is affirmed strongly, not only as a way of fostering personal formation, developing expertise in ministry and sharpening leadership skills, but there must also be more intentionality in teaching this approach as a ministry model for the congregation. The Mennonite theology of ministry includes the emphasis on "equipping the saints for ministry"; however, we have not trained persons explicitly to carry out this equipping task. Teaching the art of pastoral supervision is one key task in this agenda.

5. Mentors

Zehr assumes that the teaching program will include a combination of theologically trained professors and pastoral supervisors who are prepared to equip persons for ministry. Egli is less clear in his proposal. On the one hand, he seems to suggest that the congregational pastor is the primary equipper of persons for ministry. On the other hand, he suggests the need for a variety of courses which assumes that these would be taught by seminary professors. The confusion is created by such comments as the following:

> As the New Testament reveals, the most effective setting for training is actual ministry - not the classroom, and the most effective trainers are the church leaders - not the academic instructors.

The message in both documents is that theological and pastoral education is a churchly enterprise including congregations. As such, the mentors will not only be properly credentialed academics but will include a range of persons including members of the congregations. If pastoral education truly becomes a joint venture between academia and the covenanted community, then we will need to find ways of identifying and affirming those mentors who have not previously been recognized as teachers of persons preparing for ministry.

I have found it helpful to think of five mentoring roles as suggested by Calhoun.[2] These roles will not necessarily be carried out by each mentor with equal intensity.

Role Models

We are aware that students often reflect the values, thinking, attitudes and behavior of their mentors. The pattern of identity formation, both personal and professional, is a complex process including such things as observing (admiring) others, testing new behavior patterns, incorporating elements that fit for oneself until one feels at home with a certain style. Modeling is not only a process that happens between individuals, but it is also a corporate function. Education is also an acculturation process. For ministry it is a process of socialization into the office and role functions of ministry. It is the encoding of a common language, understanding the Mennonite ethos, community assumptions, etc. I agree with Egli that pastors should be part of the modeling; however, congregations also have a significant role in shaping a professional identity. Equipping persons entirely with an institutional/academic environment provides a one-sided emphasis in the journey of identity formation.

Authority Figures

The use of authority and power are givens in any leadership role. Part of the learning process is self-discovery in terms of who one is as an authority person and how one relates to authority. Contemporary patterns of seminary education tend to create dependency patterns in students and blunt the process of exploration which inevitably must occur. Experience-based training models help to force authority issues in a safe supervisory environment.

Companions

Companionship suggests walking alongside persons in their ministry formation. It suggests a positive relationship of trust and mutuality. The road to healthy inter-dependent relationships and strong peer working relationships is often built during the time of pastoral training. Educational models which encourage group learning, mutual sharing and confrontation are key to providing helpful models for ministry in the congregation. The TEE interactive model and the CSPE supervisory model both lend themselves to fostering interdependent learning patterns.

Educators

A significant role in pastoral formation is that of educator, passing on the wisdom of the ages. As noted in the content section, education is much more than passing on knowledge or sharing information. Part of the task is to provide tools and skills which will help the person learn from experience.

Knowledge/ideas communicated in isolation to life experiences have a low retention rate in memory and have even less impact in changing behavior or in educating for vocational roles. In other words, we should rely less on rational, linear thinking (left brain) and encourage teaching methodologies which use spatial, visual thinking and imaging (right brain) as well as emphasizing use of the frontal lobe, as per intuition, sensing, feeling. The implication is that those who seek to educate others communicate as much by who they are and how they function as by what they say.

Evaluators

Evaluations are a normal part of the educational experience. Examinations test a person's comprehension of a given subject. Supervisory evaluations are a useful tool in experience-based educational. Giving and receiving feedback is a significant element in our understanding of church life. The educational models, promoted by

Zehr and Egli, should prepare persons to utilize feedback as well as providing tools and experience for ministry in the church.

A word of appreciation to Paul Zehr and James Egli for sharing their educational vision with the church. We are in a period of ferment and uncertainty as to what directions we should go in pastoral education. They have made a helpful contribution to the ongoing discussion.

ENDNOTES

1. Clifford, N. Keith. "Universities, churches and theological colleges in English-speaking Canada: Some current sources of tension" *Studies in Religion*, Vol 19/1, Winter, 1990., 3-16.

2. Calhoun, Gerald J. *Pastoral Companionship*. New York/New Jersey: Paulist Press, 1986.

Learning Both How and What to Think as Well as How to Relate

Erick Sawatzky

There is something admirable, impressive, and encouraging about any project that is well designed, clearly focused, and efficiently executed. While I am not absolutely certain about the efficient execution of Paul Zehr's conference-based pastoral education program, the research, design, and focus lead me to believe that the execution is equally well done.

Paul Zehr's paper describes for us the components and procedures of a regional Mennonite pastoral ministry training program. He begins his work by describing the four major studies that comprise the background of this curriculum guide: biblical theological study of the pastoral gift in the congregation; Mennonite philosophy of education; extension programs in theological education; and experience-based learning. Each of these background studies is adequately and carefully described to inform the reader of the foundational components of this particular curriculum. The actual curriculum guide which follows is a logical outgrowth of the foundational background studies. The curriculum sequence is outlined and actual course descriptions are offered.

There are several elements to be affirmed here. The first is the choice of language. Paul Zehr chooses to speak about pastoral education rather than theological education. It is not appropriate to make absolute distinctions here between the two sets of terms. Nevertheless it seems clear that there is choosing to make preparation for congregational pastoral ministry more of a priority than preparation for membership in the academic guild. It seems clear that the program that Zehr outlines, while it has real academic components, is not designed to fine tune research skills, technical analysis, and sophisticated intellectual inquiry, all of which are more of a priority if one is speaking about theological education. What seems to have priority in this curriculum is a degree of scholarship in the service of ministry rather than scholarship for the sake of publication and debate. This too serves ministry but at another level.

Second, the clear identification of the target audience within the Mennonite context is to be affirmed. This is not a curriculum which claims to be applicable to all groups of people anywhere in the world. It is much more specific. It is Mennonite conference-based and targeted 1) for persons already serving in a leadership role without training, 2) for new persons who will be ordained or licensed, 3) for persons who desire continuing education for growth in their ministry, and 4) for persons who sense a call to ministry and who are identified as potential leaders who wish to test their interest or gifts. This program in a sense has done market research and has laid out a program to meet the needs of a particular market.

Third, Zehr's curriculum guide is positive and not polemical in tone. There is no hint that this curriculum is over against any other. There is no suggestion that this curriculum is better than another curriculum or better than going to a campus to study. There is no criticism of what others do. It simply lays out the background, the foundations, and the program. It is easy to read.

Fourth, there is evidence of a concern for balance in the curriculum. Clearly the focus of the study program is Christian ministry but beyond that there is clear evidence that consideration has been given to models of ministry, to knowledge of the scriptures and of the Mennonite theological and ethical tradition, to spiritual formation for ministry, to attitudes for effective ministry and to skills for ministry. It is noteworthy that so much can be packed into a relatively short study program.

For all the affirmations, there are, nevertheless, some questions to be raised about this conference-based program. I wonder, for example, whether the program is too context specific. Is the program at all transportable or is it only workable in Lancaster County? Apart from the fact that this program requires a fairly large Mennonite population base to sustain itself, I wonder whether the philosophy of education principles outlined apply well enough in Washington, D.C., the deep South or central Kansas. For example, are the emphases on Mennonite identity, peoplehood and community transportable enough to make this program work elsewhere? Along with that I wonder whether the program is too Mennonite, too separatist, and too local. It would appear that there are definite limits to the educational process and pursuits when one's dialogical partners are primarily persons who are relatively like-minded and like-cultured. There is not a great deal of opportunity in this curriculum to explore the larger world of ideas, to be engaged in conversation with persons of other traditions and of opposing worldviews and/or lifestyles. I therefore wonder how well this curriculum addresses the issues of modernity and post-modernity. It is really not very clear to me whether or how adequately this curriculum exposes students to the history of Christian thought. Do students in this program get an adequate exposure to and opportunity to struggle with the problems posed by the so-called enlightenment and its resulting spin-offs? (i.e., rationalism, foundationalism, pietism, liberalism, pluralism, etc.)

If the above is so, does this curriculum adequately prepare mis-

sionary pastors or does this curriculum focus more on the maintenance and health of the institutional Mennonite church? Put
another way, does this curriculum prepare pastors for ministering to
the broad range of needs at the close of the twentieth century? Can
persons trained in this program move beyond the confines of the
institutional Mennonite church and relate to the relativistic and
pluralistic worldview around them and function as missionary
pastors rather than maintainers of what once was?

Perhaps it is too early to answer these questions. They may not
even be fair. No program of study can do everything. Given the
thoroughness of the groundwork I am certain these questions will be
addressed.

Jim Egli has written a provocative essay on the topic of leadership training in the church. While he does not state it directly it
seems that readers are to assume he is addressing Mennonites who
have interest and/or involvement in training Mennonite leaders.

As one involved in Mennonite seminary education, I read the
essay with great interest. After all, as Director of Field Education
on a seminary campus, I am the person who advocates and symbol-
izes the practical and the "non-academic" perhaps the most. My
assignment is to lure students out of the library and the classroom
and into the congregation for learning. I believe in the action-
reflection model of learning; I believe in modeling; I believe in learning in context. But I also believe in academics and in rigorous
academic pursuits. This leaves me wondering about Jim Egli's
emphasis. To pursue these issues further I will discuss first of all
several areas of agreement with Egli. Following that I will raise my
concerns and disagreements.

First, I agree with Egli that we, the church, need to do a better
job of calling forth and training leaders. The present system which is
heavily a self-selection and information-gathering process is not adequate for the demands of ministry, pastoral or other. Hardly a week
goes by without news of painful experiences between pastors and
congregations, involuntary pastoral terminations or pastoral
dropouts. The demand for capable pastors is high. Supply is not
meeting the demand. While first class training is not the only answer
to these situations it can certainly help. We need to do a better job
of calling persons gifted for pastoral ministry in our congregations.
Then we need to do more training better than we do now.

Second, I find myself in agreement with Egli in distinguishing
between training for scholarship and training for ministry. Egli
speaks of our contemporary approach as placing "academics--the
cognitive and intellectual--at the core" rather than a life of prayer.
Whether that is the best way to set up the options is questionable but

Egli's central point rings true to me. There is a difference between the skills--linguistic, technical and rational--required to succeed in the academic guild and the skills required to pastor effectively. And there is a difference in the way one trains for working in each area. This is not an exclusive difference. Rather it is a difference of emphasis. I agree with Egli that the pastoral requires a more relational emphasis and the academic a more analytical and technical one. I would not, however, be as categorical about the values of the relational and the marginalization of content as Egli seems to be.

My third point of agreement relates to the second. It has to do with the choice of terminology. Egli's use of the terms "leadership training" instead of "theological education" finds some resonance with me. While there are problems with leadership language also, the point here is to distinguish between theological education and education required for ministerial service in the congregation. While my concern is that we not pit the academic and the practical over against each other (the academic and the practical should always be in each other's service and in the service of ministry), the two emphases stress different aspects of the learning enterprise. The terms convey a different message also. Egli is promoting an alternative to the predominant language and I find myself in some agreement.

Fourth, I agree with Egli's call for "placing training in the context of actual ministry." He offers several advantages: "motivation to learn is high, questions are completely relevant, teaching is directly and immediately applied, individual guidance and supervision are possible." These are perhaps somewhat overstated but basically I agree. In addition I would offer that training in context nurtures a sense of call, it fosters pastoral identity and teaches pastoral role fulfillment better than anything on campus. At the same time it provides the ready situation for learning the many skills necessary for effective ministry. Of course, not everything can be taught or learned by doing. Here Egli's rail fence model offers a useful way of combining cognitive learning agenda with the more practical. Nor can everything be learned on site. Presumably there is some room in Egli's model for the classroom. Or is there?

It is at this point that questions and concerns begin to cloud my affirmation about Egli's thesis. He says in his introduction that "effective leadership training is not primarily a matter of acquiring information and learning to think theologically." Rather, "it is much more a matter of learning how to relate..." Later he says, "the primary goal of Jesus and Paul was to teach potential leaders to relate" and that "the goal of the training process must be clearly relational." "It must not be seen primarily as a cognitive process where we are simply imparting knowledge and teaching persons how to think."

I really question those assertions. Yes, the word "primarily" tempers Egli's last statement somewhat but has it tempered the statement enough? I do not think so. I do not believe that the Gospels or the Epistles of Paul teach us that the primary goal of Jesus and Paul was to teach potential leaders to relate--period. Yes, they were to relate. But they were to relate a message. Content was important (i.e., love and the Kingdom of God). Jesus imparted a great deal of information. He taught the *what* as well as the *how*. Paul's letters show a similar concern. The essay would be stronger if it demonstrated as much concern about what is preached as about how it is preached.

Second, I am concerned about the apparent self-evident legitimacy of choosing certain actions and methods of Jesus, Paul and the Anabaptists and suggesting that they may be normative for the late twentieth century. Perhaps it is self-evident to others but it is not self-evident to me why one would choose to make normative Jesus' model of training his disciples but not his itinerant ministry, the choosing of twelve, his family life (or lack thereof) or his social life. Similar questions can be asked of Paul and the Anabaptists. (Note: *ME V* has quite a different interpretation of the Anabaptists' relationship to 'the priesthood of all believers' concept.) Each age has its patterns for living. Some are better than others. Renewal movements invariably challenge existing patterns of doing things. That is good. To suggest, however, that one can transfer a model of education across four, five, or twenty centuries, as well as across cultures, and make it normative seems unthinkable to me. Of course, the same problem exists with the Greek, Socratic model. That is why we need fresh, creative ways of meeting the church's needs. That requires a conceptual process as well as a relational one.

Lastly, I have a problem with the hyperbole and the polemical tone of the essay. At several points Egli overstates issues by using statements like "much more", "tremendous advantages", and "primary goal" to support his views and "elitist system" and "simply imparting knowledge" to describe what he is against.

I find it unfortunate that Egli's essay is dotted with hyperbole and sweeping statements that set content and style so much over against each other. Good points and needed corrective measures get lost that way. It is true, there are flaws in the present system of educating for ministry. Egli has helpfully identified some of them. Solving the problems and meeting the needs of this present age, however, will require learning both how and what to think as well as how to relate.

Chapter 4

The Last Word

Response to the Respondents

Paul M. Zehr

I begin my response by thanking Barrett, Bauman, Detweiler, Lebold and Sawatsky for their positive response to my work. I view them as esteemed friends who, like myself, are seeking ways to improve the quality of the pastoral ministry in the believers' church.

Pastoral education continues to be in ferment, as Ross Bender points out in the Foreword to this book. Earlier this century the seminaries emphasized Christian education, then a little later counseling (psychology), and more recently evangelism and church growth based on sociological studies (sociology) have taken center stage. As we enter the 21st century the focus will likely change again. Underneath, however, lie foundational questions: what is the gospel? what does it mean to be church and live in Christian community? what is the church's function and mission in the world? who is the pastor in the midst of the congregation? How is s/he educated?

Since my research for the thesis-project, from which my paper emerged, Theological Education by Extension has undergone assessment. The TEE Cyprus Consultation July 2-8, 1984 reported by Robert L. Youngblood (editor), *Cyprus: TEE Come of Age* (The Paternoster Press on behalf of the World Evangelical Fellowship and the International Council of Accrediting Agencies) is one example of further refinement. In the Mennonite Church and the General Conference Mennonite Church new studies of "A Theology of Ministry" are taking place. Earlier studies leading to a model for theological education in the Free Church tradition are now going through refinement. New attention is rising on theological education with a global perspective and the missiological setting for the formation of theology. During these intervening years I have also witnessed further development of Conference-Based Theological Education (CBTE), have taught several courses for pastors, and have participated in Supervised Pastoral Education for more than 80 pastors, most without seminary education. These experiences have led me to affirm the following:

-foundational, academic studies are a very important part of the pastor's education. Without it pastors lack theological discernment.

They are easily swayed by what is popular at the moment or by what seems to bring quick results without asking what theological framework the latest fad expresses. I continue to affirm the need for graduate level (seminary) education by our denomination. I also affirm biblical and theological education on the college level. And if persons are unable to attend one of these schools of higher education, I strongly affirm Conference-Based Theological Education. I agree with Richard C. Detweiler when he says, "The relevancy of theological education is not always immediately apparent, but in the long-term role of the church minister, persons discover they are drawing on theological understandings more than they anticipated they would do. Even our relationships in ministry are formulated by our theological responses to our sociological situations. Closely related also is that one's view of the church (ecclesiology) forms one's view of the role of leadership which in turn influences one's view of education/training. A church leader's self-perception and way of relating to others in ministry are theological developments for they express his or her way of experiencing God and interpreting biblical doctrines."

-skill training for pastors is a continuing need. Leadership skills, communication skills, group dynamics and conflict resolution skills, counseling and relation skills are crucial pastoral qualifications. These are enhanced through Supervised Pastoral Education. All pastors, whether seminary educated or not, will benefit from an action/reflection model of training in which they receive feedback from peers on their ministry skills. Pastors need good relational skills based on good theology. Relationships in and of themselves are not everything. If they were, congregations would choose therapists as congregational leaders. However, relationships are a very important ingredient of the pastoral ministry. Pastors can increase their skills through a supervised program of learning.

Harold E. Bauman and Richard C. Detweiler have called attention to the lack of a study course in my proposed curriculum on how the pastor trains lay persons in the congregation. I agree this is missing in the course offerings and is needed. My study was not aimed at congregational education. But on further thought pastors need training in this area to do effective congregational education. I thank Harold and Richard for raising this concern.

I also affirm Lois Barrett and Ralph Lebold in sharing their insights into educational methodology. Lois calls attention to four types of learning all of which are needed. Ralph illustrates six dimensions of the pastoral education task in the diagram. I agree with Lois when she says, "Mennonites, who have long understood the connection between knowing and doing, the inseparability of theology and ethics, can be pioneers in new models of education."

We are living in a creative time for theological education. Let us continue to learn from each other ways to improve the quality of education for pastors. In the future we will need the Mennonite seminaries more than in the past, but we will also need training within the context of the practice of ministry to enhance, not undercut, what is learned in the seminary. The academic and the practical, the cognitive and the skill sides of ministry are like twin beams without which the pastor will not survive in the 21st century. Who the pastor is, what s/he knows, what s/he does, and what his/her attitude toward the ministry is may very well determine success or failure in the pastoral ministry.

What If...?
Concluding Thoughts

Jim Egli

Thanks to those who responded to the papers by Paul Zehr and myself. You have done an excellent, thoughtful job of clarifying issues, identifying strengths and weaknesses, and adding your own insights. What I would like to do now is further clarify what I said and the key issues as I see them.

The Value of Academic Learning

I want to be clear (and I think that here the respondents have understood me) that I am not questioning the value of academic learning.

Academic learning is extremely valuable. We need Christian scholars and the academic system effectively develops them. However, I am reminding us that once we have produced a Christian scholar, we haven't necessarily formed an effective pastor (or church planter, or evangelist, or missionary). Our present system (intentionally and unintentionally) assumes that scholarship is the primary factor in leadership development. But the ministry of the scholar and the ministry of the leader differ significantly.

The cognitive is vitally important as several of the respondents have helpfully reminded us. I do not deny that, but am pointing out how thoroughly it was integrated in the biblical models with the relational dynamics of prayer, modeling and in- service training.

We should not close our academic institutions. Far from it! They can, in fact, become leaders in the renewal of pastoral and leadership training if they are willing to ask hard questions and color outside the lines of established patterns and traditional models. We must recognize, however, that a thorough integration of the cognitive and the relational dynamics of mentoring, supervision and spiritual formation will require far- reaching changes. It will mean more than adjusting a few peripheral details.

Leadership Training Then and Now

Barrett and Sawatzky questioned the relevance of the biblical principles that I put forward, because nearly 20 centuries have passed since then and now. I am glad that they raised this question because I see this as a crucially important issue. The basic question here that we must answer is this: How relevant to our task today are the biblical principles of leadership training that we discover in the

New Testament?

Perhaps this is the most important question that we must answer. Let me state it again: *How relevant to our task today are the biblical principles of leadership training that we discover in the New Testament?* Your and my answer to that will radically affect everything else.

It is true that in many ways we live in a different world than Jesus and Paul. That should affect our models and methods of training today. At the same time, I believe that the biblical principles are still relevant and powerful, even if their application takes new forms. The way persons grow spiritually, the way leadership is formed or deformed, the way a call is received and given shape, the way a vision for ministry is captured and communicated--all these dynamics essentially remain the same, then as now. Modern educational theory and research on leadership formation are confirming rather than denying the New Testament training principles.

If you think that Jesus and Barnabas and Paul have a lot to teach us today about leadership training, it will have far- reaching implications. If you think the principles they modeled and taught are irrelevant, it will mean business as usual.

Is the Method the Message?

My paper emphasized that in leadership training the method is the message. Consequently, I focused on the *how* of leadership training. Some of the respondents have pointed out that the *what* is also very important. I agree and it seems I have not stated this clearly enough. Allow me to clarify what I meant in emphasizing the method.

When I say that the method is the message, I don't mean that we simply focus on the *how* and ignore the *what*. What I mean is that perhaps the clearest and most powerful principle for us to realize from the New Testament is modeling. When we do leadership training we must realize that we are continually modeling. The question is not, "Are we modeling?" We are modeling whether we realize it or not. The question is, "What are we modeling?" When we want to develop academic lecturers, an ideal way to do that is to put our learners with gifted scholars. If we want to shape compassionate and visionary pastors, church planters, and missionaries, we will place learners with effective leaders in those areas.

That is what I mean when I say that the method is the message. Our learners will consciously and unconsciously repeat the patterns we put before them in their own ministries.

Let me illustrate it. Our present academic system models and teaches a certain set of skills. These skills overlap but are not the same as the skills needed for effective leadership. I see it this way.

 Skills needed for effective leadership

 Skills modeled and taught in a c a d e m i c schools

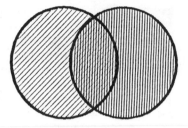

Jesus modeled the very skills, passion and values that his learners would later need in ministry themselves. By putting these before them and then involving and supervising them in actual ministry, they learned the very things they would carry forward and pass on in their own ministries. In this way, what they needed to learn for ministry and what they were actually taught were completely or almost entirely overlapping.

 Skills needed

 Skills modeled and taught by Jesus

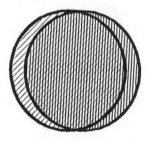

It's threatening to see modeling as primary in leadership training because as Detweiler stated "most of us are not Jesus". Never-
the-less, that fact did not stop Barnabas and Paul and others in the
New Testament from applying the same training principles. Nor did
it stop Paul from making his bold statement, "Be imitators of me, as
I am of Christ" (1 Corinthians 11:1, NRSV). Again, let me
emphasize, the question is *not*, "Are we modeling?" We are
definitely modeling and so shaping our learners. The real question
is: "What are we modeling?"

Our present academic residential system requires and models
skills that fit perfectly if the student goes on to graduate school. But
if they go on to pastoral or other leadership ministry they soon discover that they still have a lot of very basic things to learn--essentials,
like how to build a leadership team, how to create ownership for
outreach, the basics of spiritual warfare, conflict resolution, and
leading someone to Christ. Even when these issues are addressed in
the academic setting they are often not learned because the students
have not yet learned the questions that emerge from ministry.

On the other hand, in-service training unites modeling, ministry, supervision, teaching and reflection to target the very skills and
concepts needed for effective leadership ministry. In my opinion,
this is the main reason that Jesus bypassed the academic Rabbinic
system of his day in favor of his own apprenticeship model.

In many ways the method is the message. That is not to say
that the content is unimportant. It is very important. The method is
the message because it provides the model that shapes the learners'
future ministries.

A Relational Model?

I call the New Testament training models relational. What do I
mean? As Sawatzky responded: "I do not believe that the primary
goal of Jesus and Paul was to teach potential leaders to relate--
period. Yes, they were to relate. But they were to relate a message.
Content was important." His statement is true and a helpful
clarification.

I call our present training models informational because at the
core of them is study and cognitive learning. If someone can learn
the right information and think clearly, they can quite literally make
the grade. But as conference ministers and congregational members
alike can testify, some persons who pass their classes in flying colors
later flunk in relational skills.

Information was crucial to Jesus' training but relationships
were also central. "He appointed twelve...*that they might be with
him*" (Mark 3:14, italics mine). The centrality of relationships

permeated all of Jesus' training model. The disciples witnessed his intimacy with God in prayer, his compassion for the outcasts, his friendship with sinners. His teaching emphasized real love for God, one another, and others as foundational for spiritual life and ministry (Matthew 22:34-40; John 15:1-13). In-service training and supervision enabled Christ to begin correcting the disciples' dysfunctional relational skills (Mark 9:28-35; 10:13- 16, 35-45; Luke 9:54-55; 10:17-20).

The relational nature of Jesus' training was noticed by the Sanhedrin. In Acts 4 we read that they were surprised by the courage of Peter and John. Realizing that they had not graduated from an accredited school "they took note that these men *had been with Jesus*" (verse 13, NIV, italics mine). Jésus' focus on relationships echoed in his followers' preaching: "We proclaim to you what we have seen and heard, so that you also may have fellowship with us. And our fellowship is with the Father and with his Son, Jesus Christ" (1 John 1:3, NIV).

Several respondents (Bauman, Lebold, Detweiler) highlighted the biblical teaching that the role of pastoral and other church leadership is "to equip the saints for the work of ministry" (Ephesians 4:12, NRSV). The apostle Paul implies that this is the primary task of these leadership roles. Yet as the respondents point out, neither our existing model nor that outlined by Zehr specifically train leaders for this task.

Relational training as modeled in the New Testament does equip leaders to equip others because they simply continue the process begun with them. Barnabas took Paul alongside himself in ministry--encouraging, modeling and training him in teaching and church planting (Acts 9:26-27; 11:25-26; 13:1-3). Paul continued this process with Timothy and others, and expected them to carry it forward with still others (2 Timothy 2:2). Equipping persons for ministry is a relational process. It means investing time, attention and prayers in others. It requires placing confidence in them, discovering and calling forth their gifts, teaching and involving them in ministry. Leaders in the early church naturally did this. They knew how because they themselves were equipped in this way.

What are the New Testament principles?

Simply put, what are the leadership training principles that we discover in the New Testament?

1. The priority of leadership training. Study of the Gospels reveals that leadership training was vitally important to Jesus. He gave it high priority as he invested his time, attention and prayers in the future leaders of the church. We too must realize the centrality

of leadership training to the mission of the church today giving it our best planning, efforts and prayer.

2. Freedom from established patterns. Jesus and Paul freely set aside the established ministerial training patterns of their day to embrace methods that would model and equip future leaders with the very skills they needed.

3. Demonstration. Jesus showed the disciples how to live what he taught. He not only gave them a message but demonstrated how to relate that message.

4. In-service training. Jesus and Paul involved their learners in extended in-depth ministry where they could receive individual guidance and correction, where questions could be answered and learning immediately applied.

5. The centrality of prayer. Jesus both demonstrated and taught the centrality of prayer to ministry. He made it clear that the disciples' connection to God would make all the difference in the outcome of their lives and ministries (Mark 9:29; John 15:5). No matter how skilled and trained, they still needed the Spirit's empowering (Luke 24:45-49; John 20:21-22; Acts 1:8).

What if...?

One question swirls in my mind as I ponder leadership training for the church of the future. That question is, "What if...?"

What if the church at the end of the twentieth century decided to take seriously the New Testament principles for leadership training? What if pastors, church planters, conference ministers, and educational leaders together moved ahead to integrate mentoring, in-service training, and scholarly learning?

What if our seminaries ventured forth into new models of apprenticeship learning even though they knew they might not receive ATS accreditation for the next 15 years?

What if our area and provincial conferences continued to pioneer new ways of intertwining spiritual formation, ministry involvement, supervision and instruction into effective forms of leadership training?

What if pastors and congregations were gripped by a new vision for Spirit-empowered outreach compelling them to equip and release new leaders for ever-expanding ministry?

May we have God's courage, grace and discernment as together we ask, "What if...?"